ASPIRE

STANDING TALL

A Guide to Help Those Growing up Around Depression

Prologue

"I'm not fucking moving that box, it can stay where it is," said my son.

"Please move it, we need to get a sofa in tomorrow," I asked politely.

"If you ask me again I'll thump you," was his reply.

"Shall I call the Police?" says a neighbour loitering outside.

"No thank you sir, I am dealing with it," I said and closed the door.

I sat my children down in the empty lounge of our new home. The stress levels high, I felt exhausted by the drama going on around me that I was buying into.

This was yet another house move in a string of many, only 6 months after moving house before - another relationship breakup resulting in chaos disruption and the upheaval of my family once again.

Still playing the victim I was feeling sorry for myself. At this time I couldn't see that the only person causing this disruption was me.

It took a further year of challenges and turmoil for me to finally realise I was the problem. Only then could I really begin the journey of positive change and as a result watch my children blossom and change too.

ASPIRE2BFREE™

STANDING TALL

A Guide to Help Those Growing up Around Depression

Positive change happens when you become aware of NOW and begin to take steps towards loving you

Written by

Sarah Haywood

First Printing: 2017

ISBN: 978-1-9997563-0-7

Published by:
Sarah Haywood
Aspire2bfree
www.aspire2bfree.com

Dedication and Appreciation

This book is dedicated to the memory of my brother who is mentioned within this book and whom I love dearly.

I would like to express a huge thank you to my children, parents, friends, boyfriends and all those who have shared experiences with me along my journey so far. It is these experiences that have inspired me to write this book. Without you I would not be who I am today.

Thank you to my daughter Georgia Haywood for creating the front cover illustration and one within the book.

You have been given the gift of life. How you choose to spend it is your choice.

The greater your awareness of YOU, the bigger the potential you have to live a happy and fulfilled life.

Disclaimer

This book is written from personal life experiences shared to help others who have lived through similar events. The views and opinions are that of Sarah Haywood based on her own personal experience. They are not intended to be a substitute for medical advice from a Medical Practitioner. You should consult with your doctor or a qualified specialist in any matters regarding your mental or physical health that you are concerned about.

Sarah Haywood is a Spiritual Growth Mentor providing guidance to those seeking it based upon her own experiences and understanding of the physical and non-physical. Her aim is to help you appreciate and love yourself better so that you have the opportunity to lead a more purposeful and fulfilled life.

Foreword by Derek Mills

Invest the time to read this book. Why?

Until I was 38 years old, I was struggling in my self-employed business. I had an inner depression. I never even once told anybody about it and I didn't seek help. Knowing what I know now, I wish I had. But wishing does not make things come true.

Taking action is the only thing that does this.

I spent most of my life crouching down, hiding from the world and hiding my true gifts, causing myself, and those around me to suffer immeasurably.

I know the pain of not loving one's self. I know the anguish of not feeling loved by others even when they absolutely did love me and were committed to me beyond what I realised.

I am blessed to know Sarah Haywood now, yet I would have given anything to have come across her work in this book when I was in my 20's and 30's.

Being part of 'Think & Grow Rich', the biggest brand in personal development over the last 100 years, has taught me that the business of helping others, via a book or any other medium, is about authenticity and principles wrapped in a story that can absolutely help those who invest the time to read.

I met Sarah in 2012 and found her to be real. No fake gestures or trying to be something other than her true self. This authenticity appeals to me whenever I feel or see it in anyone. I remember when I first spoke for her organisation it was so easy to just

BE myself and to share what I had inside. Sarah 'held that space' for me then.

Through her works Sarah has helped thousands of people find their truth and a better way to live their life. I know she is 'holding a space' for you now, as you continue to read Standing Tall.

This book 'Standing Tall' contains real stories, about love, life, career, family and money - All the areas vital to holistic success. Moreover Sarah writes in a way I love to read, authentically and as if she is speaking directly to me. I love it when a book does that, don't you?

You will find the pathway to your truth in this book. We can only be happy as our true self. So prepare for greater happiness and prepare to begin to love yourself even more.

I recently filmed my part in the mega-movie Think & Grow Rich the Legacy. I wasn't always wealthy. Wealth came late in life for me. However, I know what it is like to be poor, poor of heart, poor of spirit and poor financially. As a featured expert in this movie and with 20 years' experience in wealth management, I am so pleased this book Standing Tall also includes real world solutions to the problem of money, careers and business. I'm grateful because this is the real world.

There is dark as well as light. There is lack as well as poverty. There is struggle as well as euphoric moments. The struggles make us. The euphoria doesn't last. What lasts is 'us', the very essence of who we are, when we grab life, demand the best of ourselves, but accept and still love ourselves when we fall or fail.

For this, life is about getting up, standing up, Standing Tall, as yourself, your true self.

If you read this book and follow the guidance contained therein, you will gain that which is promised in the author's introduction.

Derek Mills *Best-selling author of 'The 10-Second Philosophy®' & Expert in 'Think & Grow Rich - The Legacy' Movie*

W[illegible] which we gain [illegible] demand the best of [illegible], not accept [illegible] and still love ourselves when we fall.

[illegible] standing up [illegible]

[illegible] and follow the guidance [illegible] gain that which is [illegible]

[illegible]

ASPIRE2BFREE™

STANDING TALL

A Guide to Help Those Growing up Around Depression

Contents

Introduction

As a child everything you experience becomes your world.

I grew up with my parents and a brother who was just 15 months younger than me. Most of the time we lived a normal existence. There were ups and downs, some of which were extreme, but to us it was our way of life.

One of my parents suffered with depression and still does today. This affected and continues to affect their self-esteem and as the years have rolled by it has also created high anxiety within.

When we were young this sometimes had a knock on effect onto my other parent causing challenging moments to arise. As a result, the environment created gave me an unsettled feeling within, making the home sometimes an unpredictable place to be. As a sensitive child this left me often feeling alone and in need of love and reassurance.

Unable to see their own self worth, despite being extremely talented, the parent affected by depression was rarely able to share any positive feedback on things I did. This had a knock on effect on my self-confidence and became the role model of what to expect for myself.

Whilst in school there became an acceptance within myself that I was to be treated as someone of not much interest. Being a sensitive child and a redhead I was easily upset by negative comments made to me by others and as a result I became an easy target for them to be cruel to.

As I grew up this became my world - I didn't question it or see it as anything other than normal.

As an adult the boundary was set. The limitations of such an upbringing meant that my outlook on the world and what I thought was possible for me was based on a low self-esteem and lack of love for the self.

Over the years I learnt to draw those close to me that were of a similar belief, attracting friends and boyfriends suffering some kind of depression. After all this was the setting of normality I was used to.

Looking back I can see how easily a child can be drawn into a way of being. How those around them are imperative to setting the parameters of what will be their expectations for life.

Before I woke up and became aware of what I had become, I brought 3 beautiful children into the world. Each of them experiencing similar limitations because of the parameters that were set within me and in the partner I had attracted.

In 2002 the dissatisfaction within me erupted and I chose not to accept this life any more. I had no idea where I was going or how I was going to change things. All I knew was I needed something to be different in my life.

Leaving my husband I stepped onto a rollercoaster - my children strapped tightly on with me. Going from relationship to relationship I searched for the answer to finding happiness within me, believing each time this would be what I was looking for.

In 2011, only then did I truly wake up. 8 years of challenging times later.

Each relationship had stirred something up. Emotionally I was a wreck. I needed to change my life and a light into the darkness came. It came into my awareness that I was the one who needed to change before the contents of my life could become what I wished for.

It was then I experienced a spiritual awakening - a time of unearthing some deep truths about the world and my true purpose. I became aware of things that I had never even thought about. My eyes were opening to something new.

Since that year I have been learning new ways to live my life. Ways to truly love who I am and to break the pattern of living within the parameters of depression. Although I have never been diagnosed with depression, I can recognise now that the effects of living around it had begun to define me and I was living within the boundaries of it.

It has taken me a further 5 years to finally see the truth. To unravel the mystery of why things within my life have been so limited.

This book has been written to share with you my journey and how I have managed to overcome these boundaries and open my heart to a new life. It shows how I have begun to explore and enjoy my sensitivity allowing me to accept and love who I am.

It offers guidance and tools that aim to be of help and comfort to you if you have also experienced similar things.

We are what we choose to be. My choice is to be free to be me.

Some Information About Depression

In many countries of the world those suffering with some kind of depression or mental illness is increasing. Within the UK and United States alone there are 1 in 4 people who suffer.

Depression is an illness that affects the energy of the body and mind.

Each person consists of energy - in fact that is all we are. If you imagine your own body as a bag of energy, within it there will be pockets of good feeling energy and sad feeling energy. I see these as sad and happy faces.

Each of these faces has been formed by the experiences you have undergone throughout your life. As your life progresses these pockets of energy build up. If they are not recognised, eventually the sad faces rise to the surface and show themselves as illness or pain within the body.

For some people the experiences they have as a child are so sad that the sad faces become overwhelming and this defines who they are as a child. This can greatly affect their childhood and how they see themself within it. If the child is not given any help with this, the sadness within will have a negative impact on their adulthood until they become aware of this and choose to change it. You may recognise this about yourself.

Not only does the body react to experiences but it is also affected by what is absorbed into the body through the environment.

Particularly within the western world, this is very apparent. Children are subjected to high frequencies in the atmosphere from mobile phone signals, Internet signals, vibrations from television programmes and computer games, food that has no nutritional value, drinks that are full of sugar, caffeine, and much more.

Everything that you experience as a child and adult whether physical or emotional is interacting with you in some way.

For example, think about when you are watching something on the television. If the programme is negative and carrying negative messages, your body will start to absorb the low vibration. You are likely to reach out for food and drinks that match this vibration as a comfort. This is a likely time when chocolate, crisps and alcohol or fizzy drinks in particular are consumed.

If you are watching something of a higher vibration that makes you feel good, such as a musical, comedy or educational, it is likely that your energy will rise with it. The food and drinks that you consume here, especially if these types of programmes are watched regularly, are more likely to be healthier to match the higher energy that you feel.

Depression is the result of lots of sad faces congregating together to form a deep sadness within you. Over a period of time this sadness becomes overwhelming and it is difficult to be without it.

There is no single cause to depression. It is can be a combination of many things. Some of this can be put down to a chemistry imbalance in the brain, genetics or an imbalance of hormones.

Other things affecting it may include:

- A lack of self-love creating a low self-esteem
- Anxiety disorder, borderline personality disorder, post-traumatic stress disorder (PTSD)
- An experience of physical or sexual abuse
- Gender mismatch - feeling like you are in the wrong body
- Chronic diseases like diabetes, multiple sclerosis, or cancer that result in a person feeling negative and sad
- Alcohol or drug abuse causing a depressive state to emerge
- Being a sensitive child and adult who is easily upset by others
- Certain prescription medications causing an imbalance within the body
- Family history of depression - learnt behaviour or genetically transferred
- A sense of feeling different - not fitting in with the norm

To be diagnosed with depression will usually mean you have suffered with it for more than two weeks and are displaying at least 4 symptoms of the disease:

Some symptoms of depression include:

- Extreme irritability often over a minor thing
- Anxiety and restlessness
- Anger - an inability to control it
- Persistent frustration with life and others around
- Lack of interest in things or people around you
- A fixation on the past and what has gone wrong or what is missing in your life
- Constant negative thoughts about yourself and others
- Hating yourself because your body is the wrong gender
- Thoughts of death or suicide
- Often feeling upset by other people's comments and behaviour

Some physical symptoms may include:

- Insomnia or sleeping too much
- Fatigue to the extreme that you can't do anything
- Affect on your appetite - either eating lots or very little
- Weight gain or weight loss

- Lack of concentration
- Inability to make decisions
- Unexplained aches and pains

Children affected may become very anxious, withdrawn, clingy to parents and unable to deal with going to school

Teenagers can become very negative and reclusive

Depression can lead to:

- Alcohol or drug addiction and abuse
- Headaches and other chronic aches and pains which affect your mobility
- Phobias, panic disorders, anxiety attacks
- Getting into difficulty with school or work
- Family and relationship problems
- Social isolation
- Comfort eating resulting in weight problems or obesity
- Anorexia due to a lack of and no desire to eat
- Self-harming such as cutting, extensive tattoos, piercings - anything that creates pain
- Addictions to things that make you feel better such as sugar, painkillers, fizzy drinks, and caffeine
- Erratic or disruptive behaviour caused by an unsettled feeling inside
- Attempted suicide or suicide

To not deal with depression in some way can therefore result in very serious consequences. It will eventually have a negative impact on your own life and those around you.

Those who are affected by growing up or living around depression may not have the symptoms in such extreme ways, but their behaviour and energy levels will be defined by the effects of being subjected to the symptoms.

You may find yourself suffering mildly with depression. You may not feel the need to seek treatment for it. If you choose to do nothing to change it, the effect will be to limit your life and your thinking, consequently impacting on your future.

A Glance into Depression

By Alison Bavistock - February 2017

Invisible Illness

Laid in my bed, outside rain beats down
In the dark of night, I contemplate life
The dreams I never found, sadness surrounds me
For what should have been, time that's wasted
Depression took from me

Some days, I wish
I could flick a switch, and be no more
I have died inside, the tears have gone
Empty of emotion, taking a day at a time
The fire within me, gone for now

People ask, how are you
I say I'm fine, they don't want to know
My mask, the smile, that's what they want
They can't take the truth of how I am

The 'tears of a clown'
That's my song
Nobody sees behind closed doors
Life moves on,

People absorbed, in the drama of life
They just don't see, the likes of me

Overcoming the Effects of Growing up Around Depression

As someone growing up around depression, it is not always obvious that you have been affected. Your life will seem normal to you. You will have come to accept this as the way your life is going to be.

To want to change your life means that you have come to a point within it that has become uncomfortable. A time when you no longer wish to accept the way things are and you are ready to consider a new perspective.

If you have reached this point, you will find this book has been written for you. Having been on a journey of change for some years, each step of the way has given me an insight into the difficulties you might face on your pathway to change.

I have chosen to write this book in a way that reflects both the old and the new me. The reason for this is to allow you the opportunity to resonate with aspects of it so that you have the possibility to see how each experience you may be encountering could be perceived in a more positive way.

I have chosen to breakdown the book into sections of my life. Each section deals specifically with the problems I faced and how I sought to change my perspective on them. If any of the areas identified are particularly difficult in your life at this time, this would be a great place to start reading. You may find that some go hand in hand together and you naturally progress to another section. If like me all areas of your life are affected, you may find reading the whole book from start to finish of some comfort and benefit.

Before going into the sections I want to talk about a set of actions that have particularly helped me. I call them **The Safety Zone**. As you go through the book you will hear this referred to and examples have been given showing how I have applied it.

Throughout life you will experience many things. Your perception and reaction to such experiences is unique to you. They will be based upon your upbringing and other influences that have affected you throughout your life. If you are to create a different perception and consequently a new response, first you have to change something in the way you deal with each experience.

Where your childhood has been affected by living around depression, your perceptions and expectations are likely to be based on the boundaries set by this experience.

To change means to first become aware of what is happening and how you are responding. **The Safety Zone** gives you this opportunity.

The Safety Zone™

The first part of **The Safety Zone** is to **STOP**.

If you liken this to a red traffic light, this instructs you to stop in order to allow other traffic to carry on around you. This is effectively what you are doing.

Red also represents the Base Chakra in your energy system. This chakra's purpose is to help you become better connected with the earth and what it can offer you. It guides you to become grounded so that you can see the reality of your life more clearly and bring all you need to survive into it. (See **Appendix 3** for more information on this chakra)

When you find yourself experiencing something that is beginning to make you feel uncomfortable, **stop** what you are doing for a moment and take a deep breath in. If necessary take a few deep breaths. By breathing in deeply you will bring oxygen to the brain and to your organs. As you do this, your body will automatically become calmer.

If you think back to a time when you were stressed in a challenging situation it is likely you will remember your body became tight and your breath more shallow. This would have been your fight or flight reaction - that of survival.

By taking the time to stop and breathe deeply your reaction will change. Instead of fight or flight you will give yourself time to consider your response.

When the mind is obstructed by emotion it is

unable to think rationally. Its only reaction is to come from a state of emotion that in turn brings with it an emotional response. Often this will not be the reaction you would have had, had you taken the time to stop and consider things before responding.

The second part of **The Safety Zone** is to **OBSERVE AND LISTEN.**

If you liken this to an orange traffic light, this instructs you to get ready by watching and listening to the circumstances around you before moving off.

Orange also relates to the Sacral Chakra in your energy system. This is the chakra to work with when you have limiting thoughts and feelings around change and are struggling to let go of old habits connected to these. (See **Appendix 3** for more information on this chakra)

Once your mind and body is calmer, you are able to step into your rational mind. This step allows you to take some time to **observe and listen** clearly to what is happening.

If for example a child is screaming in a public place, by stepping into the orange part of **The Safety Zone** it will allow you a moment to clearly see the emotional state of the child and the surroundings you are both in. You will have time to locate a rational response to the situation.

If you respond without stepping into **The Safety Zone**, the likelihood is that you will react from an emotional standpoint based on a personal viewpoint. Your emotional response to this may result in shouting as a memory of hurt from the past creates your reaction. Stepping into **The Safety Zone** gives you time to see your own personal reflection upon it and change your response to be more personal to the child before you.

You may not have much time to step into your safety zone. However, the more you practice this, the easier it will become.

By taking the time to see the reality of any situation rather than remembering your own past experiences automatically alters your response. It gives you the opportunity to treat each person and situation uniquely rather than taking the actions of others personally. This in turn will give you a chance to help them through the situation rather than adding to the drama with your own emotional response.

The third part of **The Safety Zone** is **GO**.

If you liken this to a green traffic light, it suggests that now it is time to put into action whatever your conclusion is after observing and listening to what is happening, provided you feel safe to do so.

Green also relates to the Heart Chakra in your energy system. Your Heart Chakra helps you to see a more loving perspective for yourself so that you can see past negative thoughts and feelings lingering in the mind. (See **Appendix 3** for more information on this chakra).

At this stage your mind is clearer and your response more astute to what is happening - you are present rather than lingering in stories from your past.

When you reach this state of awareness you are connecting entirely to the now moment. Only when you become aware of your own self and what is happening in your mind can you change old thinking patterns. Coming out of the mind into your heart will help you to bring more loving responses and feelings into your life.

To begin with you may need to step into **The Safety Zone** for a longer period of time, though some situations may not allow you time to stop for long at all. The more this way of behaving becomes a habit the quicker your rational mind will leap into action and your old way of being will disappear.

To remind yourself how it feels to be outside **The Safety Zone**, think about a time when you responded irrationally to a situation and it escalated out of control. Now remember how you felt afterwards when others were hurt by what was said.

Emotions come in all kinds of disguises:

Positive Feeling Emotions

1. Joy, knowledge, empowerment, freedom, love, and appreciation
2. Passion, inspirational
3. Enthusiasm, eagerness, happiness
4. Positive expectations, belief

5. Optimism, encouragement
6. Hopefulness, patience
7. Contentment, harmonious, peace

Negative Feeling Emotions:

8. Boredom, fatigue
9. Pessimism
10. Frustration, Irritation, Impatience
11. Bewilderment
12. Disappointment, disillusionment
13. Doubt
14. Worry
15. Blame
16. Discouragement
17. Anger
18. Revenge
19. Hatred, rage
20. Jealousy, lust
21. Insecurity, guilt, unworthiness

If you are feeling any of the top 7 emotions, it is likely your reaction to things around you will remain positive. This is because these feelings are coming from a loving place and as such will create loving experiences.

If your feelings fall into the emotions 8 and below your reaction is likely to be negative. This is because these feelings are fear based. Since this is the case, the consequential experiences are likely to match this.

Learning to bring your energy and mind-set into the top 7 on a constant basis can take time, especially if you are not used to feeling this way.

As you learn to change your mind-set life begins to match your new outlook. Each positive new habit that you install into your day will eventually cause a knock on effect into all aspects of your life.

Below are the sections I mentioned earlier. Within them you will see some of the positive new habits I have found that have helped me. The more I have implemented them and become aware of myself, the greater the changes within my life have begun to reflect this. The happier I am becoming the less concerned I am about my future.

'Que sera, sera' - what will be will be - how I deal with experiences will determine what will become.

MY LIFE STORY SO FAR

Self Love

My Story as I saw it then

There is no doubt that when you are entrenched in your life and living in the shadows of the past it is unlikely that you will see through the story that surrounds you.

As a child growing up I found it difficult to love me. Looking in the mirror everyday I would compare myself to others. I believed everyone around me was better than me in some way.

As children at school tormented me about the colour of my hair and called me mean names, I began to believe them. This together with the effects of living around depression caused me to withdraw emotionally, losing connection to any love I might have felt for myself.

As I became needy of love from others because of what I lacked for myself, I found myself always wanting to please - desperate to seek support from others because I no longer knew how to support me.

By focusing on the ugliness of how I felt about me I gained a low self-esteem and lack of confidence in myself. All I could see were the shadows casting over me. There were moments when I triumphed in something I loved which brought me some joy. However, when positive things were said to me they often trickled off me like water on a ducks back. It was difficult to accept words from others that I never said to myself.

When I got married I became sad by the lack of love that my husband appeared to be giving to me. I felt alone and trapped within a marriage that felt cold.

When I left my marriage 14 years later I thought that love existed in a good passionate sexual relationship, something that had been lacking for sometime.

By setting out to rescue others who needed love I thought it would give me a purpose within a relationship - a need to be needed. This was fine until the quest was fulfilled and the time came to move on. This resulted in a string of intense relationships based on the wrong reasons that became difficult to extricate myself from.

Jobs came and went as I moved myself on as I reached a certain point of success within them - always keeping myself within the limitations that were familiar to me. Each time I moved I started a different type of work, causing me to start from the beginning again with my earnings. This led to debts and difficult times financially.

With every part of my life remaining unsettled, it was a reflection of how I felt inside.

My Story as I see it now

Reflecting back over my life I can see that each step I was taking lead me closer to the answers I needed to hear so that I could change my life for the better.

Looking back at my childhood it is now clear to me that those around me were simply reflecting back to me the way I saw myself by their responses towards me.

Each role model in my life brought experiences to me to enable me to learn something more about myself. My reaction to them being the reflection I needed to see.

It is clear now that the marriage and love relationships I have formed over time have been based on a need to be needed and loved. It was the deep lack of love and confidence in myself that caused me to seek approval from others as a way of distracting myself from the reality of what I felt inside.

No matter how much others offered to love me, their words were heard but not felt. It taught me that it was impossible to accept love from another until I could love myself. The words they said felt superficial. The previous history of hurt that I was carrying meant the wall around my heart was almost impossible to penetrate, placing myself in my own prison.

This way of viewing myself created circumstances around me which were reflecting my own story back to me. Only when my awareness changed was I able to see this for myself. It took many relationships, each one becoming more challenging and hurtful to walk away from before I finally realised what I was doing - that the problems being created were my own creation.

Once I recognised this and the need to change me, I began to view my life and all the relationships within it differently. It gave me an opportunity to get to know the real person that I am rather than the person I had become.

By freeing myself from employment and becoming self employed it enabled me to explore many aspects of myself. It gave me the opportunity to break free of old habits and things other people have said about me. It has encouraged me to turn inwards and explore the essence of who I am. This in turn has unveiled a wrath of creativity within myself that before I had denied the existence of.

By exploring myself I have discovered love and a connection to a greater power within me that before I never knew existed.

Without the experiences that I have encountered and the challenges I have faced I accept I would never have understood that my life could be changed. Therefore, I can now view them in a positive way rather than feeling sad about them.

The continual uprooting and unsettlement meant that change was inevitable for no one changes anything standing still.

The effects of living around depression as a young girl meant surrounding myself with others who were the same. Consequently, many of the friends and boyfriends I have attracted into my life have all suffered some level of depression.

Looking back I can see now that anyone who was not of this energy did not fit into my world and my need to be needed.

When I consider my career path I can see from the constant upheaval that I was in fear of success. This fear was a reflection of the lack of love I carried within me. Where there is no love fear resides instead.

For the majority of my life I have played the victim. Always believing it was somebody else's fault that I hadn't yet found happiness within. Yet how can anyone else ever be responsible for my happiness? They are not me and can never be me.

It is clear to me now that no one truly knows the experiences any of us has had. We all look at the world through our own eyes, hear through our own ears, smell through our own noses, taste in our own mouths and feel with our own bodies. Everything we experience is therefore unique to us including our thoughts and how we view the world and others around.

This has led me to finally see that I am responsible for my own reactions. That how I respond to others in the world is a reflection of how I truly feel within and the consequences of my responses are mine alone.

Instead of pleasing others, it is therefore much better to be honest to myself, and honour how I feel. Every time I tell a lie to myself I tell it to others too.

If you lie for too long, eventually there is an explosion in some way. Honesty is always the best policy as they say.

We are each therefore the victim of our own way of thinking.

Recently I have understood that what I think I create. It has led me to discover that our minds are a very powerful tool. Such a discovery has changed my life. Focusing on the lack in my life has always led to a lack. Simply by changing my outlook I am now able to appreciate all that I create by appreciating the power my mind has and me.

The Law of Attraction, talked about in the next section of this book, states that what we focus on we create. Consequently negative thoughts about you will inevitably lead to negative experiences in order to fulfil this prophecy.

Below are some of the tools explained that I have found to be useful in helping me learn to love me.

Tools I have used to help me

To help me gain love for myself so that I could finally be free of my past I have experienced many things that have contributed to this. Below are some of the most helpful:

Emotional Freedom Technique (EFT)

After leaving my marriage each love relationship that I encountered over the next 6 years drew me closer to feeling more and more unsettled.

As my emotions cried out to be healed I looked around for something or someone to help. In 2009 I discovered a technique called Emotional Freedom Technique (EFT for short).

This technique was like magic. It enabled me to release old negative emotions that were deeply entrenched into my belief system and to build a new confidence within myself.

Using the theory we are all made of energy I discovered that each experience I had undergone in life had imprinted itself into my belief system, my memory, and my energetic body. It was this that was affecting my thoughts and behaviour.

If you liken yourself to a computer, when you were conceived your hard drive became activated. Every experience since your conception has written a new programme into your hard drive. As you have grown up, you have automatically drawn on the resources of this hard drive in order to live your life. You know exactly how to respond to circumstances because the hard drive has recorded it. Another name for this is your subconscious mind.

EFT is a tapping technique that deactivates these programmes. By tapping on Meridians (energy portholes on the body) you can release the stagnant and trapped energy representing these programmes, allowing your computer to realign itself and be open to new data.

EFT has had astounding results on many people. It can be used for releasing anything negative that is affecting you, especially pain, phobias, memories, grief, negative beliefs and thoughts, old habits etc. It can also be used to enhance and encourage new habits, positive thoughts, creating new programmes for better health. (See **Appendix 2** - The Basics of EFT for further information)

When I first started to use this technique my self worth and ability to love me was very low. My energy was filled with lots of sad faces after experiencing one difficult challenge after another. As I started to tap on the meridians I found myself releasing old self-sabotaging beliefs based on my childhood. I began to see that a lot of how I had been responding to life was based on a set of thoughts and behaviours that were so ingrained within me, I had no way of seeing them for what they were.

EFT helped me to refocus my mind and thoughts and to become aware of ways to begin to love and nurture myself more. It gave me the clarity I needed to move forward in a more positive way.

After using EFT for a while on myself, I began working with clients. As this developed I found myself experiencing messages and images that were from the client's loved ones who had passed over. This made me inquisitive and drew me to explore my spiritual self. I had delved under the surface of my emotions and discovered a centre of knowledge that was to further change my life.

Meditation/Mindfulness

This led me to explore meditation.

Until now I had dismissed meditation as something that was not for me. Every time I sat down to try, thoughts would simply never stop. If you have ever tried, you will know exactly what I mean.

After attending a spiritual awareness course locally, I was drawn to become aware of some more energy points on the body called chakras.

It was explained to me that each chakra has some relevance to different aspects of our lives. If any of these are blocked or damaged the impact on the energy you have for that aspect of your life will be affected as a result.

For example, the Solar Plexus provides us with the energy to have self-love, confidence, self-belief and self-value.

When these points are blocked or overwhelmed with sad faces/negative energy, they become unbalanced and the energy that would normally be there to help us in this aspect of our lives becomes limited or dormant.

It was when I unblocked the chakras and became aware of them that my life began to change further. (See **Appendix 3** - Chakras and their meanings for further information).

Having unblocked my chakras I felt drawn back to meditation and as I did my experiences changed overnight.

As I enjoyed sitting quietly I experienced colours and white light and a sense of pure peace. Each time I meditated different things occurred. Sometimes my arms and head were encouraged to move. It wasn't frightening as the space I found within was peaceful and loving. Instead of my normal gesture of ten minutes I was now spending an hour or two hours in meditation.

After about a week I had an extreme burst of sexual energy emerge in one meditation, which I later became aware of as a Kundalini experience. This occurred because of my wish to give birth to the energy of Christ into the world.

These experiences for me were a spiritual awakening and so the responses I was having to meditation were part of a special time in my life. Today when I meditate on a daily basis, it is more to bring focus into my life. Sometimes this is deeper than others.

For you it is likely that meditation or mindfulness, depending on which route you choose, will be to help calm your mind and bring your focus to the present moment.

(See **Appendix 1** - Meditation/Mindfulness for further details on how to begin using these techniques).

Mindfulness is slightly different in that it guides you to focus on a particular thing so that you can increase the awareness of your thoughts.

The ultimate would be to stay in a state of awareness - the state you reach in mediation - within all parts of your day. However, only those who are persistent and consistent in their practice are likely to achieve this.

Being in the NOW

As I have increased my meditation practice the more often I have found myself connecting to and being aware of what I call the 'Now Moment.'

Having experienced the effects of being asleep and that of being aware, I can honesty say today I appreciate and accept the only thing that exists is NOW. It is clear that once the past has gone it cannot be changed and the future has yet to appear. Therefore the only place we have any influence on is the present moment of any day.

Looking back I can see I spent a lot of time thinking about the past and what happened during it. It meant my focus was no longer in the present. My thoughts were also often pining for a better future, taking precious energy away from creating in the present day I was in. Both of these scenarios were limiting the time I could spend enjoying each day and what I had right now.

As I brought my awareness into each day it became easier to make changes in my life. At last I was able to see the reality of my situation rather than putting my head in the sand.

The Safety Zone became a very useful tool to me, teaching me to come back into the present moment even when a storm was happening around me. It taught me to stand tall and see everything more clearly before making any reaction to a situation.

Having created an image of low self-esteem for myself based on my experiences, the only way to change the image was to become aware of it. When my focus was on the past or the future, my awareness was vague and old patterns of thought were able to thrive.

Channeling/Inner Sanctuary

Two weeks after the spiritual awakening began I had the sudden urge to sit in front of my computer and begin to type. Closing my eyes I allowed whatever words wanted to come to pour out onto the page.

Over the coming 3 months, when time allowed, I wrote 3 big messages - each one profound and deeply moving. It was a privilege to be given such an opportunity to experience this wonderful event.

Each message was profound and filled with wisdom inviting us as humans to consider our lives here on the earth. The first message was called The Philosophy of life - A deeply moving piece about the earth and how negative it has become. Half of it is written in normal writing and half in prose. The second message was called The Philosophy of Love - A beautiful poetic journey explaining what unconditional love is in great detail, profoundly worded, totally resonating with me. The last one was called Why are People afraid to use the word God? - A controversial title revealing some wonderful thoughts on who and what God is. These can be found on my website:

http://www.aspire2bfree.com/free-articles-to-download.html

Each of these pieces deeply moved my soul and made me think about my life at a deeper more profound level. At this point I wanted to go out into the world to share these messages, but quickly realised over the coming year that first I needed to walk my talk. The messages were not only intended for sharing but were also to open my awareness to what I needed to do in my own life if I was to truly live an authentic and happy life.

Since then I have come to realise that each of us is capable of tapping into this deeper connection within ourselves. This was not something unique to me. Within each of us there is an inner sanctuary that is pure love. This love is a connection with God, for God is love as I discovered through my messages. Some of you may not like the word God so instead simply imagine your inner sanctuary filled with love - a part of you that speaks only the truth from a loving place. This is a very special sanctuary that gives you the opportunity to understand your life from a more profound level.

It has been shown to me that I am creating everything around me along with others through the thoughts we are each having. This is the same for you.

By connecting to this inner sanctuary you have your own special connection to a universal love that holds information that will help you on your personal journey. This universal love is what connects us all. As you find a solution to a problem for yourself involving others, you find it for them as well.

If everyone were taught to connect to this inner sanctuary from an early age, life would be made so much easier since everyone would be focussed on love. The desire and dedication to speak and act only from love is all the inspiration you need to connect to this place within you as often as you would like. Meditation will enhance your ability to stay connected to this place increasing the positivity in your thoughts throughout your day.

These messages led me to look at my life, my belief systems, thoughts and feelings. By becoming aware of the judgments and expectations I had of myself and others I was able to take responsibility for my own happiness at last.

This new awareness took me on an exciting new journey that led me down many pathways, exploring things that I would never before have been open to. The limitations I had subjected myself to became clearer as new boundaries were reached.

Angels

A new adventure began when I discovered angels. Beautiful beings of light interacting with us to help us live a life that is based on love - a perfect combination for someone whose journey was clearly in need of understanding the power of unconditional love.

This was a wonderful moment in my life. As I grew more comfortable working with their energies I began to channel messages from them and Ascended Masters.

After a while three of the angels came together through me to channel a trilogy of books, filled with messages of love and advice to the human race. It was an honour and privilege to bring these pieces of work into the public domain.

If you would like to find out more about these books and others, please go to:

http://www.theangelwhisperer.co.uk/books-for-sale.html

The first e-book in the Trilogy, Manifesting a Better World is free.

Working with the angels has taught me to learn to let go and trust in all that is around me. It is clear to me now that we are not alone on our journey. When we take the time to connect to our inner sanctuary there are others within the universe that can reach us at that time if we choose to connect with them.

When you focus on love you draw close to you those that match these thoughts and feelings. Angels are a gift from God to help you on your journey and consist of nothing but love. Their help is completely dedicated to you in that moment. They have no way of judging you, nor do they have any expectations of you.

It was a wonderful discovery to find out that every one of us has a Guardian Angel by our side. Your Guardian Angel has been with you since your soul came into existence. (See **Appendix 4** - Angels - for more information).

Life is full of possibilities. As I have opened my mind to allow in new thoughts and a greater awareness, new doors have begun to open.

In the past I had limited my thinking and awareness and as a result limited my life. My ability to see beyond my thoughts kept my experiences limited to one challenge after the next. Nothing in my consciousness at that time brought my awareness to the universe and those that are unseen around us waiting to help us when in need. Instead the limiting thoughts continued to stay in my head mocking me each day.

For example, imagine yourself going to post a letter. What would happen to the contents if you simply went back home and placed it in a drawer instead of posting it? There would be no response from the person you intended it for since they will never be aware of what you had to say.

Now liken this to your thoughts. If you hold onto a thought so that it rattles around in your head daily, how can anyone else in the universe help you if you leave no space for new thoughts to come? How can things change if you constantly hear and think the same things over and over again?

To create new thoughts and feelings you first need to let go of the old thoughts. As you do it gives the universe the opportunity to guide you to experiences and people that will show you how to enhance or change what is wished for, depending on whether it produces a positive or negative feeling outcome. Signs that remind you of something, words, books, conversations all add to helping you see a perspective that will help you. Angels, if asked to help, will be behind some of what comes.

Another analogy might be an artist standing at their easel with a blank sheet of paper. The artist knows exactly what they want to paint as it is implanted in their mind. However, until they paint it no one else can share in their vision. If they never painted it, the image would become extinct. If a vision is not shared or taken out of the head and expressed somewhere, it simply loses its power to be created. Instead you will receive signs from the universe of procrastination and confusion around you as your mind is clogged with visions that are left only to your imagination.

It is usually self-doubt that stops such thoughts becoming a reality. The energy that you will be portraying out around you will be negative as your dreams are left unfulfilled.

To explore the power of your thoughts, think of a time when you thought about a person and within the same day they contacted you in some way. The energy of your thought entered the universe and the person you thought about picked up on the energy.

This can be likened to a radio signal. When you turn on the radio you can hear sounds and vibrations. Your thoughts are the same. Each thought has its own wavelength. It enters the universe and connects into those that need to hear it. If you have invited angels to help you, they will gladly do so if you let the thought go and stop worrying about whether it will be answered. Trusting in them and their ability to help you will allow you to get on with the rest of your day, letting go of negative feeling energy and focussing on the positive things that are happening.

For me, I have often had thoughts about something I would like and within the same day or week it has appeared. Flowers have been a particularly good example. One day recently I saw a person delivering flowers across the road. 'How lovely it is to receive flowers I thought.' That evening I was holding a gathering and one of the attendees brought with them the most beautiful bouquet of flowers for me. It was an amazing feeling knowing that with just one thought I had created something so magical. I thanked the angels for listening.

This is only a small example. The power of your mind is phenomenal. Working together with angels and other light beings can enhance this power and help you to flow more freely within your daily life.

Their help is always based on unconditional love - trusting this and knowing this will give you the confidence to let go of the worry and see in the solutions that are shown they are here to support you. This leaves your mind open to focus on loving thoughts consequently raising your vibration and leaving you feeling lighter and brighter.

Imagine what changes you could bring to the world if everyone focused on the same loving thought at the same time. In fact I am sure you can name some changes within society around you that have been the result of this.

Examples of historical events are, earlier in the 19th Century women being allowed to vote, 25 years ago the Berlin Wall being taken down, the end of World War 1 and 2, the end of the Apartheid in South Africa. For all of these events to occur many would have put thoughts out into the universe that this be their wish. As they did their thought waves congregated together to form the solution that resulted in the outcome. Together with those unseen in the universe, the power of the wavelengths formed the final result.

If you have the power to change the world it is most definitely possible to change your own life. Experience has shown me that simply becoming aware of your thoughts gives you the opportunity to change. By connecting to the angels, it enhances your ability to get extra help and support ensuring a more loving outcome.

Learning to truly love who I am by becoming aware of my thoughts and connecting with angels, beings of light, has given me the opportunity to learn to love others unconditionally. This has changed my perspective from lack to abundance. Now that I focus on the abundance of love in my life by appreciating loving things that happen within it, it allows love to flourish in all areas of it. Previously focusing on a lack simply turned the flow off and created more lack.

This new approach has enhanced my ability to attract new people and situations into my life that are in line with what I desire. Instead of compromising and finding my life unfulfilled I can honestly say I now enjoy being who I am. This is a huge gift to myself and has had a knock on effect on others around me.

Appreciation

Learning to appreciate my life as it is and the people in it, has renewed my energy for life. It has created an opening for me to explore my creativity.

With a new confidence I have been able to explore my gifts and talents and discovered my passion for writing.

Although I had attempted writing previously, my lack of confidence, self love and self-belief denied me the possibility of doing anything with it. Instead it remained hidden until my spiritual awakening began.

To help you see what your own thoughts are reflecting into your life, think about a time when life felt particularly difficult. That might even be now.

What did or do you focus upon? The likelihood is that your mind was or is drawn to all the things that were or are lacking in your life at that time or now. This focus would have drawn or is drawing more of what was or is lacking into your life. This was or is likely to be creating situations that were or are even more challenging. I know this to be true because I can see the pattern in my own life.

The Safety Zone

To stand tall and allow the storm to happen around you means to first be aware of the situation and all that is happening. This is where **The Safety Zone** comes in handy. By stepping into **The Safety Zone** you have time to assess the situation, to come out of your emotional state and into your rational mind. Once in the rational mind it is much easier for you to see the solutions. By focusing on the solution you will draw your thoughts away from the problem and begin to feel more positive as a result.

For example, when you find yourself lacking in confidence, your mind and body become deflated. You become nervous and anxious about the situation before you. Stepping into **The Safety Zone** gives you the opportunity to gain clarity. By calming your emotional state you can connect to the rational mind. In this place you can reason with yourself.

Nerves are usually based on a previous experience. Stories that are spinning around in your mind that tell you this situation or person is going to cause you harm in some way. By stepping into the rational mind you can adjust your thinking by releasing the emotional tag that you have created and focusing simply on what is happening in the now moment.

EFT is a great tool to use at this point as it has a calming effect.

If you have not learnt to love yourself, it may be that your own insecurities still interfere with your responses since this has become your permanent emotional state.

However, the more you use **The Safety Zone**, the easier it will become to recognise each insecurity for what it is. As you get to know these old habits, you can learn to change them and the stories around them. This in turn will change your response to situations that previously reminded you of them.

Crystals

Another tool that I found to be useful for me was the discovery of crystals. These are beautiful pieces of natural formations that are gifts given to us by the earth.

To help with self-love I have found Rose Quartz to be of particular use to me.

The more connected to my inner sanctuary I have become, the greater my ability to feel their energy has grown. (See **Appendix 5** - Crystals for more information about crystals).

Summary

Learning to love you is a journey. Each day is an experience given to help you discover the truth of your own beliefs.

There are no wrong or right ways to live your life. Your choices will determine the experiences you have. Accepting each experience and learning to stand tall within them so that you can get the best from all that is happening, will guide you to a more fulfilled life.

If you want a more loving experience, first you must acknowledge yourself and learn to see yourself in a more loving way.

Loving you frees your mind. No longer will you have the same expectations of love from others. Instead you will feel stronger within yourself. This will unleash a new power within you to express yourself more freely and allow you to enjoy being who you wish to be rather than who others think you should be.

Clearing negative thoughts about yourself based on past experiences from your mind will enhance your capacity to be loved and to give love to others.

What you focus on you create. Thinking negative thoughts about you will create negative experiences to reflect back to you what you are thinking.

Changing your view to one of love will attract love into your life.

Things you can do to help yourself

Not all of the tools that I have used will appeal to everyone.

Recognising that everyone is unique, what tools work for one may do nothing for another. The important thing for you is to work with what you feel drawn towards. If you find a tool to be useful, this will indicate that it is of some benefit to you. For me personally it has been a combination of many tools that have helped me.

Below are some simple things you can experiment with that aim to help you begin to learn how to love you:

1. **Cameraperson**

Become the cameraperson in your life for a week. Spend time observing everything that is happening in your life. Notice the people who surround you and the way they behave towards you. Observe how much of your life is fulfilling and which parts you are doing simply because you feel you have to. Notice how you are feeling and whether your energy is high or low.

By observing yourself and your life you can begin to be aware of what it looks like in reality and the thoughts you are having as a result of it.

2. **Journal**

In another week buy yourself a fresh writing book - a

journal. Each day write down how you have been feeling throughout the day. Write out all the highs and lows. If you are in pain, note down how much pain you have experienced. If you are feeling unloved, notice where you are seeking love from and who. If you are lonely notice what your response is to people when they approach you. If you lack trust, notice your feelings and where they originate from.

This awareness will help you to see how you are contributing to the way you feel by noticing your reaction to situations and people.

3. **The Safety Zone**

Once you have become aware of yourself, practice using **The Safety Zone** for a week. See how many times you are able to change your response by standing tall and letting the storm be around you and not in you.

4. **Meditation/mindfulness**

Spend 10 minutes a day practicing some kind of meditation or mindfulness. I have given an exercise for both in **Appendix 1**. Note down in your journal your thoughts and feelings about yourself during this.

5. **Creativity**

Spend some time doing something creative. If you feel you are judging the outcome and not able to do something as a result, explore it using EFT. (See **Appendix 2** - The Basics of EFT)

6. **Emotional Freedom Technique**

Every day spend 15 minutes using EFT to help you eliminate some of the negative thoughts you are having about yourself. Be consistent on those that are deeply rooted. Consistency creates less resistance and a greater chance of change.

Examples of statements you might use are:

Even though I struggle to love myself, I completely love and accept myself

Even though I feel ashamed of my past, I completely love and accept myself

Even though I feel like I am in the wrong body, I completely love and accept myself

(See **Appendix 2** - The Basics of EFT for full details of how to use)

7. **Affirmations**

Write out a couple of positive affirmations. (See **Appendix 6** for more details). Say these to yourself both morning and night.

8. **I love you**

Put a photograph of you somewhere in your home where you will see it every day. Every time you look at it say: "I love you." This may feel strange at first. However the more you practice it the easier it will become.

Once you are able to say "I love you" to your photo practice saying it to yourself in the mirror.

Look yourself in the eyes and say, "I love you." Say your name afterwards so that it strengthens what you are saying.

Be consistent and persistent and you will succeed.

Health and Wellbeing

My Story as I saw it then

Throughout my life I have been consistently lucky that physical illness or injury has generally eluded me. I have always believed within me that I carry an army of special soldiers that take action whenever any kind of illness comes near.

However, when I was 17 I did contract glandular fever, which took me to my bed for a couple of weeks at a crucial time of exam study whilst at school.

When I gave birth to my first child by C-Section, I remember feeling very lonely, sad and unsupported as I was left alone in a strange hospital whilst my son struggled in the neonatal unit for the first few days of his life.

After my third child my husband and I managed to split a condom during sex. Immediately he insisted that I should take the morning after pill. It was one of the most difficult decisions I had to make since I could sense I was pregnant. With my heart breaking I took it and spent a day in bed as a result.

When I felt the need to end my marriage, every part of me felt worthless. It felt like I had failed, forcing me into a search to fulfil a need to succeed. This led me on a journey of constantly seeking approval and needing to feel loved. Mentally my mind was constantly filled with negative thoughts and feelings of frustration. This led to many times of feeling sad, lonely, unsupported and unfulfilled. I remember crying lots. Some might say I was depressed.

With my first boyfriend after my marriage I became pregnant at a point when I knew inside the relationship did not feel right. Plans were forming in my head of running away with all the children as soon as was possible. However, sadly at 12 weeks I miscarried and so the decision was taken out of my hands.

Alcohol and caffeine were things I would often use to perk me up in the short term whenever I felt down.

Exercise was something that happened occasionally. It was not a priority for me since I was lucky enough not to carry too much excessive weight as I was constantly on the go.

My diet was what most people would see as normal in the UK, eating meat and vegetables, bread and cheese, crisps, fruit and nuts, Chinese takeaways, pizza etc.

Boyfriends came into my life that would comment about food, wanting to be stricter with their diets, which at the time I found to be irritating, believing them to be fussy.

Once when I organised an event with a friend who was vegetarian he wanted all the food to be this way. I felt horrified as I felt sure meat eaters would find this to be off putting.

Sometimes I would get extreme headaches - mild migraines. My automatic reaction was to take

Paracetamol or pain killers and sleep them off believing this was the only way to rid myself of pain.

My Story as I see it now

During the time before my spiritual awakening I would not have questioned any of my behaviour with regards to my health. To me I was living a normal existence and did not believe it to be a particularly unhealthy one.

Having the mind-set that I have of strong soldiers who help me to keep illness away has certainly helped to keep me from falling under the spell of illnesses that could have continued to a deeper level, had my mind-set been different.

Having learnt a lot about the power of the mind more recently, I can see that even before I was awake, I was aware of the power of suggestion and focus.

For example, think about when you have a common cold. What do you focus on? If you spend time thinking about the symptoms and how you feel, your mind creates more of it. The reason being, your mind is focusing upon it.

If you are prone to colds yearly, you may be pre-programmed as to what to expect. You may start with a sniffle, gain a cough and end up with a chest infection. This pre-programme immediately begins to play as soon as your cold symptoms begin, creating the same outcome time and time again.

Contracting Glandular Fever when I was 17 taught me that illness when it comes can be very debilitating, despite my greatest wish to be free of it. It allowed me to have some kind of understanding for those who suffer such debilitation each day.

As part of my spiritual journey I have learnt that the body works in mysterious ways. Some say over 87% of illness that we contract is an emotional response in the body in some way to alert us to the emotional difficulties we are not wishing to face at the time.

Louise Hay, in her book Heal Your Life, talks about this in greater detail. She has at the back of her book a list of illnesses and emotional responses that are attached to them that she discovered as part of her work. Using this I can see that Glandular Fever relates to the anger of not being appreciated and loved. If I had known that then, I could have worked on it with the tools I now have. However, since my awareness was still limited I simply had to experience it as it was.

When I gave birth to my first child, the feelings that I had are not uncommon for someone left unaccompanied by their family in a strange place at a time of vulnerability. Now I can see that this experience was to reveal to me deep emotional feelings that I had lurking within me. However, at that time I was unable to appreciate this and the feelings instead led me to feel negative around a time I had been so looking forward to.

When I look back on my marriage and the relationships that followed, I can see that the focus of my mind led me into situations that created even more of the difficulties I felt. What I focused on I created and as a lack of support and love continued to be what my mind saw, this is what became my reality.

When my husband and I had the accident with a condom and he asked me to take the morning after pill I collapsed inside. He was rejecting the possibility of expanding our family something that I was happy to do. It felt like torture having to take the pill. We clearly had a different view of what we wanted in our lives.

Now I can see that had I been stronger within myself I could have said no. I can also see that to create a child it is much better if both parents agree. However, his choice at this point put us on different pathways from then on. This taught me that we are each responsible for our own actions. That no matter what another wants, if you feel strongly about something you have the right to do what is best for you. It is impossible to change some decisions once they are made.

When another opportunity came to have a baby it was with mixed blessings. The situation and partner were not right but the idea of a baby was a gift. It was a particularly stressful time when I lost it and so it is not surprising that it didn't stay.

As a mother losing a baby, no matter the circumstances, it is something you never forget. The memory always remains. However, using EFT has helped me to remove any emotional hurt around the memory so that it no longer holds a negative effect on my wellbeing.

Some of the relationships following my marriage were particularly challenging and alcohol became a way to fix the problem. Red wine would often help to null my true feelings and allow me to be more amenable. Looking back I can see that this happened more than I realised.

The lucky thing for me is that alcohol actually makes me feel ill very quickly, so I was never likely to do myself too much harm with it.

Sadly I can't say the same for my brother, who tragically died only last year at age 46, his body no longer able to sustain the damage from the alcohol he drank. It is likely that he saw no difficulty in drinking alcohol for the damage was unseen until it showed itself as illness.

Having seen the photos of my brother kept by friends and a video of him when he wasn't drinking, I could see that the two people were different indeed. On alcohol he was the jolly man full of jokes everyone came to know. Without it, he was sad and empty, no emotions on show.

My brother was not interested in changing his way of life and in the end died as a consequence of the way he chose to live.

As part of my spiritual journey I gave up alcohol naturally about 3 years ago. I found that I no longer needed it as I had learnt how to handle my emotions better and have been quite happy existing without it since.

As for caffeine, I am sure many of you will relate to using caffeine as a way of perking yourself up in the morning especially. I used to drink 2 or 3 cups of strong black coffee a day.

Not long after my spiritual awakening I suddenly woke up one day and decided I no longer wished or needed to drink it. From that day on I have not craved coffee or drank any. A couple of years' later normal tea also disappeared from my diet.

It is clear from these experiences that when my mind and body are ready to be in sync with certain thoughts and feelings, it automatically rids me of habits that no longer suit my current thoughts on wellbeing.

Forcing yourself to stop eating or drinking something often makes you want to do it more. Think how many times you have given up something and gradually found yourself eating or drinking it again - sometimes a gentle persuasion by another or a stressful moment. If the trigger for the behaviour has not changed, the behaviour will show itself again either by repeating the same thing or finding something else to replace it.

This is often why smokers end up eating more when they choose to give up. Their habit is simply replaced by another, neither of which is healthy for them. The reason is that the unhealthy thoughts and feelings are still lodged in their mind. Until the old pattern of thought is removed and replaced with another it will always find a way to be fulfilled.

The more I began to clear my mind from negative thoughts, the greater my desire became to eat healthier.

For about a year I thought about giving up meat, feeling guilty each time for eating the flesh of another living animal. However, the taste of it and the enjoyment I got from it kept luring me back to it.

Until one day I channeled a piece of writing from my inner sanctuary about the way animals are currently treated on the earth. It talked of how an animal's energy becomes negative by the ill treatment that it receives during its life. How on death the animal is in fear as it senses its own demise no matter how kind the slaughter. It went on to say that during many livestock's lifetimes often toxins are pumped into them to make them grow faster to fulfil our growing demand for meat. It was then I realised that not only was this a cruel way for us to treat animals that trusted in us as humans but that I myself was absorbing all the fear and negativity within the meat as I ate it. A few days later I decided I no longer wished to eat meat and have not been tempted since.

Admittedly I convinced myself that fish was ok for a while, but have since drawn the same conclusion on this. I haven't gone completely vegan yet, as I am not consciously totally feeling in alignment with this. However, I can feel my awareness and feelings drawing me to consider this as I continue on my spiritual path.

It is clear now to me that my irritation with my vegetarian friend when organising our event was all based on my own feelings of fear. His comments simply accentuated my fears about giving up meat.

This new way of eating has led to other things changing in my diet (details are given below for those interested). This has made me aware that the feelings of irritation with my boyfriends over food were again my own fears of change. It took several years before I finally accepted that change was ok and a positive thing for my health and wellbeing.

Looking back at exercise I can see that I was in denial. Surely being slim meant I was fit enough without having to go to a gym or run a mile or two. After all as a single mother of three I was convinced that being constantly on the go was enough.

It was a boyfriend that made me aware of my errant ways and invited me to try adding exercise into my day. After a while of defending my behaviour I grew curious. Funnily enough it was after we split up that I finally decided to give it a go, much to his frustration I am sure.

When I think about it in energy terms, when we run or exercise we are inviting the energy within us to flow more freely. When we don't the energy becomes stagnant and we begin to feel lethargic and more easily agitated. If certain parts of the body are not exercised they lose their elasticity and become harder to use. If I was going to be healthier with my diet it did not make sense to neglect the rest of my body and so it was logical to begin adding some form of exercise into my day.

Meditation, as explained previously, has really helped me to focus my mind. By meditating first thing in the morning before I exercise it helps to bring peace to my mind and draw my awareness to anything that needs my immediate attention in that day.

Many entrepreneurs also do this - having put it into practice I now understand why. Since adding these new disciplines into my life, my mind has become sharper and I find it easier to concentrate on one thing for longer periods of time, something before I found difficult.

Now that I am meditating, my diet is healthier and I am exercising my headaches have become rare. When I do get them, I no longer take painkillers. Instead I observe what is happening in my day that has created such an irritation in my body. It has become automatic to think about what foods I have been eating or what stress I am putting myself under emotionally which may have contributed to it.

EFT (See **Appendix 2** for more details) is a brilliant and easy tool to help relieve pain. If this does not work for my headaches, I have found spending time closing my eyes and relaxing until it passes helps. Usually these days it is lack of sleep that causes it and so this is when I have to admit a little extra sleep is needed to cure it.

Painkillers are handy if you need to quickly numb the pain, but I have found they are not the answer or cure. They allow you to walk past the emotional reasons the pain might be there. If you do not take the time to understand why it arose the negative energy that caused it will persist within your body until another time.

Since my body is the only vessel I have for this lifetime, I have chosen to nurture it the best way I know how. Now that my awareness has opened to this new way of being it makes sense to pursue it whilst my mind-set continues to create a happier and healthier life for me.

Tools I have used to help me

Meditation/Mindfulness

Meditation/mindfulness has helped me greatly in learning to become aware of negative thinking thoughts. As I have become aware of them I have been able to work through them and alleviate myself of them, gradually reducing them one by one. This has enabled me to turn my thoughts around to more positive feeling ones that are now changing my life for the better.

To experience the real benefits of meditation/mindfulness I have now completed two ten-day silent retreats with Vipassana. This is an organisation that teaches people how to meditate in a certain way that brings them peace of mind, body and spirit. The great thing about the Vipassana organisation is that you can attend these retreats for a small donation - what you can afford. Their mission is to teach as many people as possible this wonderful technique and so they rely solely on donations of money and time to exist.

Although I don't practice their way of meditating all of the time, I do find it to be very powerful and useful. It has helped me to connect to the reality of each day and still is something I am drawn towards when I can.

Morning Routine

One of the things that have changed permanently for me is my morning routine. It has become a valuable asset in surmounting change in my life.

Hot Lemon

When I first get up, after feeding the cats, I make myself some lemon water. This is hot water with a slice of fresh lemon in it. This helps to cleanse my body ready for a fresh start to the day. It has been mentioned that it is also good to have this last thing at night allowing the body to cleanse overnight.

Admittedly I still like a hot oat or rice milk before bed so I haven't yet incorporated this, but it may be something you might like to think about.

Meditation

After my lemon water or sometimes whilst it is cooling, I spend half an hour to an hour meditating, depending on the time available. (If I get up early enough, I prefer to do an hour).

A comfortable way to do this I find is sitting on my sofa cross-legged with a blanket around me. However, you can sit cross-legged on the floor on a yoga mat if this is preferable to you. When practicing Vipassana they always sit on the floor unless people have back or limb problems. In these cases they are allowed to sit in a chair.

The trick is not to rest your head on anything otherwise you will simply fall asleep.

(See **Appendix 1** for more details on meditation)

Exercise

Although I exercised when I was younger, recently I had fallen out of the habit of doing it.

To begin to change this I started walking first thing in the morning - walking to the count of 30 and running to the count of 30.

It was surprising to me how easily I became out of breath. It made me more determined to keep going. There are two fields near to where I live and these served a great purpose in getting my stammer up. Soon I was running the whole time.

To save my feet getting wet every day, I have now found a route that still takes me near to trees but on drier land some of the time. Sometimes I run for 20 minutes and other times 40 - it depends how much time I have in that morning.

On a Saturday morning I have discovered there is a Park Run nearby - something that is available in many areas of the UK. This is an opportunity to join others for a 3K run. I have done this a few times, but prefer for the time being to run by myself. However, now that I have renewed my passion for running (as I used to run as a child) I intend to join them more often as I would like to complete a marathon one day. Although this seems a huge leap from where I am now, it is good to have ambitious goals to strive for and this is an exciting prospect that I would love to achieve.

When I run I find that my mind becomes sharper. It has been particularly noticeable to me at Governor meetings in the evening, since I have been able to follow and understand the content better rather than being too tired to do so.

The fresh air revitalizes me and helps my body and brain to function much easier.

It has been brought to my awareness the importance of spending time in nature. The energy that nature shares with us is pure. This helps us to detox and get rid of negative energy that is often holding us back.

Sometimes I now choose to do some other exercise either instead of or as well as in the mornings to help stretch and tone my body.

Stretching and toning helps to keep the body supple enabling me to stay and feel younger. Yoga is a combination of mindful movements that stretch the body gently, making it less stressful on the joints. It relaxes the mind at the same time as working the body and keeping it supple.

There are many types of yoga I have discovered. If you feel drawn towards it, try out some different ones to see which is most suited to you.

Very recently I have discovered that I have damage to the inside core muscles called Diastasis Recti due to multiple pregnancies. This has now required me to take a different approach on my core exercises. I have realised that each of our bodies are different and it is important to do what suits you and yours if you are to get the best results.

Juicing

When I get back from a run or finish my exercise I often have a fresh vegetable juice to help boost my energies and give me a healthy start to the day.

At first the juice tasted strange but as time has gone on I find it tastes great. A typical juice for me these days is:

2 carrots

1 beetroot peeled

Some celeriac or celery

1 lemon

A piece of fresh ginger

A piece of fresh turmeric

1 Apple

Sometimes some spinach or broccoli

A spoon of Spirulina/pea protein

A spoon of Udos Oil or Virgin Olive Oil

Having spoken with a nutritionist I have discovered that juicing acts faster than smoothies when injecting nutrients and goodness into the bloodstream.

Smoothies are great, acting as a food supplement but the body has to work to digest them first before the goodness hits the bloodstream. They make a great breakfast alternative. However, you might like to have a juice shot first to help energize you more immediately.

Change of Diet

Since giving up meat my body has become more sensitive.

After a while of this change, I found my energies plummeting to a low ebb on a regular basis.

To help rectify this I went to see a Homeopath (Holistic Practitioner) who told me that I had a mild intolerance to gluten, dairy and sugar. For the next two weeks I knocked these out of my diet to detox myself. After this he did some work on me using kinesiology that has since allowed my body to tolerate small amounts.

My choice now is to eat gluten, dairy and sugar free when I can. However, admittedly my taste buds still enjoy some of the foods that contain these and so I allow myself moments of digressing. Sometimes this is fine and other times my body shows me reactions that make me stop to question myself as to why I felt the need. Usually these are on more emotional days when old habits creep back in. The digressions are getting less as I clear my mind of negative thought and feelings. However, I have realised it is important to go with the flow and not beat myself up when I do. Life is for living and each day brings different experiences and as a result requires differing sustenance.

Since changing my diet two of my children have begun to become more aware of theirs. Both have become vegetarian and one has now declared herself Vegan.

Now that we all have different dietary requirements, the children, now adults prefer to cook for themselves, choosing what they want to eat. At first I found this to be difficult - the need to stay in control element of being mum. However, I have learnt to relax and let them be free in their choices.

Part of the reason for feeling fearful of this change was that previously I had not enjoyed cooking just for me. It did not seem worth the effort so I would often choose easy convenience meals if the children were not around. This was a shame since I have always loved to cook.

Since learning to love and take better care of me, it has become important to eat healthily too. Whether I am cooking for just one or several the pleasure of cooking has returned and I have fun experimenting with new things.

From the observation of others and myself, it is noticeable that we are what we eat. When we are feeling negative and low we reach for unhealthy foods - usually processed and non-living foods matching how we feel. When we are feeling high and positive we eat healthy foods - usually fresh and alive matching the feelings we have.

It has become apparent that many children are being born into the world allergic to many of the foods that are currently more difficult for our bodies to process. Meat, dairy, gluten and sugar are amongst these. As the parents of these children learn more about the effects of these foods on the body, they become more willing to consider the changes for themselves also. As their awareness grows they share the knowledge discovered and a domino effect begins.

Appreciation

By learning to appreciate myself I have begun to care more for my health and wellbeing.

Learning to appreciate my own wellbeing has given me the inspiration to change my diet, exercise and meditate, seeing them as something important to my mental and physical health.

This has opened my eyes to the habits of my children and enabled me to steer them towards healthier practices where I can.

It has helped me to appreciate my body and to take better care of it. My new awareness has shown me that the body is an important vessel that carries us through our lives. If we neglect it, it begins to affect and limit our possibilities.

Illness can be very debilitating. If you are someone who suffers a lot, beginning to change your habits to more positive ones will help. Remembering that the law of attraction insists we attract what we focus on, become aware of your thoughts and their focus. If your symptoms are problematic and have become your focus, understanding the emotional aspect of why they might be there, could be a way to help you see past them. Become aware of where the label for the illness came from. Is it something you have grown up with? Think back to when the symptoms started. What emotional difficulties were you having at that time or a few months before? Is it a label that you have come to accept and live within? Once you see an emotional link or the dialogue that keeps you focused on it, you can use EFT to help relieve you of the negative impact it is having. It may not completely rid you of the illness but it may begin to start you on a road to recovery as your focus and energy change.

This may not work for all illness. However, along my travels I have come across many who have dramatically changed their life by changing their focus on the illnesses they had, taking them out of wheelchairs, removing severe pain, mending broken bones etc. If illness is the bane of your life, it may be worth checking out some of the success stories for yourself.

Appreciating that all experiences have consequences within your life will help you to become aware of them more. As you appreciate each experience as a learning event, it will help to steer your focus to clear any negative data that occurs more immediately. Using **The Safety Zone** will help.

Acceptance

To enable change it became apparent that accepting responsibility for my own emotions and feelings was imperative.

Whilst my mind was focusing on the things that were lacking in my life, it encouraged more lack to occur. My energies dropped and I became sadder inside.

Meditation/mindfulness enabled me to become aware of these thoughts and feelings. As I became aware it gave me a choice whether to continue or to change them.

In order to change them, first I had to accept and take ownership of them - I had to take responsibility for my life and what I was creating within it.

Once I was able to accept this truly from the heart, it allowed me to forgive others and myself. It helped me to understand who I had become and to see how I had fallen into this trap of negative being. For the first time I was able to see my life clearly and define how I now wished it to be.

This new focus gave me the inspiration to begin to believe in new possibilities. No longer did I feel stuck on this pathway. At last by accepting responsibility for my own happiness I was able to readjust my thoughts accordingly. This readjustment has led to better health in all areas of my wellbeing.

By accepting who I had become I was able to forgive myself for the challenging experiences I had created in my past.

This was a very important stage of being able to let go of the past and all the hurts that had occurred along the way.

Affirmations

To help keep my mind focused on the positive aspects of my life, I found that daily affirmations helped. (See **Appendix 6** - Affirmations - for more details)

Affirmations are a way of programming new thoughts into the mind so that they become real. With regards to mental and physical health this means creating sentences that express how healthy and well you are. A few examples might be:

Everyday I am healthier and healthier

Today I feel great

In this moment my health is in perfect divine order

My thoughts and feelings are positive today

I love and enjoy being me

One affirmation I created which I like to use is:

I love my life

I love me

I love the world

I am free

Although not health related per se by loving the world and me it creates a feeling of happiness and consequently good health.

Remembering that your databank is full of old sayings and information that you have learnt throughout your life, the use of affirmations helps to override these. If used often they become your new way of thinking and being and will have a positive impact on those areas of your life you wish to change.

Emotional Freedom Technique (EFT)

EFT, as mentioned earlier, is able to help you to readjust your energy, removing old negative feelings, thoughts and habits.

EFT is therefore excellent for helping with your health.

EFT can be particularly useful whenever you experience some kind of pain.

For example, I remember having a particularly bad toothache. After several rounds of tapping with EFT I found that the pain went. Although the pain was gone the reason for it still remained. It was therefore still important to visit the dentist who later performed a root canal on this tooth.

Not all pain that is alleviated leaves behind a problem. Having worked with many people to help rid them of their pain, two stand out. Both of them, at different times had pain in their shoulders and expressed limited used of them as a result. Both had tried different treatments including a Chiropractor.

Working with EFT I asked a few questions which led to finding the core reason behind the original pain - in both cases it was an emotional response to something which had happened in their life. By working on this core emotional issue the pain went quickly and easily. Both now have full pain free use of their arms and shoulders again.

If you have some kind of allergy or difficulty with food there may be an emotional reason for this. Sometimes it is the programming you have given to yourself based on your current beliefs. If this is the case, ask yourself first whether you wish to change it or if you prefer to keep this belief. If you choose to keep it the allergy will remain as a response to your new way of thinking.

For example, you may wish to eat dairy free in which case your body will continue to react if you have any. This will be because your energy will become more sensitive to it and treat it as a toxin, bringing your awareness to it so that you are reminded not to eat it again or reduce your intake.

If you have suffered some kind of trauma in your life, EFT is able to penetrate deeply into the body to release whatever responses are trapped within your energy. This can take time if it is deeply rooted. However, once one layer has been removed, it allows another to be revealed. As they say, it can be likened to peeling back the onion to reveal what is inside.

Trauma can show itself in illnesses that penetrate deep into the tissues of the body often causing pain and suffering as a reminder of what you encountered. EFT will help to release the suffering around the memory and as a result the suffering that is now your reality.

Angels

For those of you who are curious about angels, I have found them to be invaluable in helping me undo old unhealthy habits and releasing negative beliefs from my mind.

Archangel Raphael is known as the healer. He can be called upon to help you with your health and any pain. The colour associated with him is green. This is a peaceful natural colour resonating with all that is natural.

One way to call Raphael is simply to say his name and ask or you can expand your request further as follows:

Dear Archangel Raphael thank you for helping me to release this pain in my--- (putting wherever it may be in this space) and bringing my awareness to anything that will help me to resolve any emotional difficulty that this is a result of.

You can choose how you wish to word your request to him. The idea behind thanking him is to assume that the deed is already done. Remember that what you focus on creates the response. If you focus on the pain, more pain will come. If you focus on the solution, Raphael can work his magic and help it to disappear.

The Law of Attraction

Understanding the law of attraction can help to alleviate a lot of things in your life. Every experience of things that are lacking creates some kind of emotional response, often a negative one.

To learn to change this so that your focus is upon the solution means to understand why this is important.

Within the universe there is a rule called The Law of Attraction. This rule is universal and cannot be changed or altered in any way. For me, if something cannot be changed it is best to learn it so that I can benefit from it rather than suffering from my own ignorance.

As the words 'Law of Attraction' suggest this relates to attracting things into your life.

For example, if you focus on getting a job because you lack a job, your focus is on the lack of a job and not the new job. This attracts a lack and no job appears. This is why people often say it is easier to get a job when you are in a job.

Why is this? Think about the artist mentioned at the beginning. If you were an artist focusing on the desire for a job you would paint every detail and become excited by the prospect of doing exactly what you paint. You would use bright colours and your energy would be that of joy. The more you paint the easier it will become to see what you want.

Now imagine focusing on the lack. Your energy would be low causing you to see nothing but darkness. You may not even be able to paint anything. Any colours you would use are likely to be dark and dismal and the energy that you would hold is likely to be that of sadness. This would limit your ability to create anything at all.

The Law of Attraction responds to energy. If your energy is that of joy it can be likened to music that is sweet and harmonious. The more harmonious it is the greater the likelihood of it being in tune with what you wish to create. If your energy is sad the music will be sombre and low and the signal consequently low to the ground. This is likely to be so heavy that it dissipates before it can reach anything.

Relating this to health and pain, think about the last time you had an ache or pain in the body. How did you feel? Was your mind focused on it? Or did you null it with painkillers so that it had no effect? Or did you simply carry on with your day ignoring it but still being niggled by it? If any of these, the pain is likely to have continued.

If however you were able to use **The Safety Zone** and spend some time observing the pain, you would become aware of the reality of it. If you were able to see it as simply energy your awareness would know that this pain must be temporary and will go when it is ready since energy flows when blocks are released.

Accepting the pain and being aware of it but not paying attention to it will allow your mind to focus on other things. The more you change your focus, the less the pain will throb.

Nature teaches us that nothing in life is permanent. Once your awareness is in alignment with this belief, you can release the focus and change the direction of it with your thought. Consequently this will override what the mind thinks and the pain will dissipate.

Think of stories you have heard where people have persevered through difficult circumstances despite breaking their leg or arm. Their desire to survive taking over any thoughts of pain they may have. The broken bone still existed and could be fixed whenever possible. However, the pain was overridden by the stronger desire to survive. Their focus became that of survival and therefore the law of attraction was able to deliver the solution to this desire rather than staying focused on the awful situation they were in.

Crystals

My knowledge of crystals is very limited. However, I have found that when I need one to help with the solution of a problem, they appear in my life.

One such crystal is Amethyst. This is a purple crystal that has properties enabling it to help with clearing negative energies. By holding such a crystal you can release negative emotions that are upsetting you.

When I find myself in disagreement with one of my children, and forget to step into **The Safety Zone**, I find my mind wandering into the old territory of taking what they said personally.

Taking time to hold my Amethyst crystal and close my eyes helps me to refocus my mind and see the truth of what has happened. The crystal works its magic by connecting with my energy and bringing any negative feeling energy to the surface. As I forgive myself and focus on a peaceful outcome my body together with the crystal's energies release the negative feeling. Sometimes this can take longer than others depending on the deepness of the hurt.

There are many crystals all with amazing properties that can help you with your health and wellbeing. There are many experts on this area who have also learnt how to do therapies using crystals for healing health problems. The Internet is a great source of contacts and information if you feel drawn to this. (See also **Appendix 5** - Crystals for some basic information on crystals).

Summary

Health can sometimes be taken for granted, especially if illness has often eluded you. Becoming aware of your eating habits and general wellbeing can help you to ensure this continues.

Building a regular routine into your life that incorporates meditation and some kind of exercise can help to increase your energy and rid you of negative feeling thoughts.

Be patient with yourself and your body - change takes time. The important thing is to be persistent and consistent with what you are doing. A new habit takes 28 days to form. Once formed you are more likely to stick with what you have chosen to do even if some days you slip back into old habits. The new habit will have become ingrained in your mind-set and will remind you of what you need to do.

Being aware of your emotional state and using Emotional Freedom Technique to work through any upsets can help you to prevent illness.

Accepting that you are responsible for your own wellbeing and learning to appreciate your body will help you to maintain a healthier lifestyle.

Archangel Raphael is known as The Healer and will bring you healing if asked. This relies on trust and faith and the desire to connect with this loving being.

Things you can do to help yourself

Below are some ideas of ways you can use to enhance the way you look after your health and wellbeing:

1. **Mindfulness**

Spend time observing your body. Close your eyes for ten minutes and observe all the sensations that are occurring during that time. Notice your breath, how relaxed or tense do you feel? Take note of any sensations of pain or discomfort. Become aware of your mind and what thoughts are processing.

After ten minutes write out what you observed.

2. **Emotional Freedom Technique**

If you observed pain or discomfort, practice doing some EFT. This will help you to accept the pain or discomfort and to bring focus to what may be causing it. Think back to when you first observed the pain happening. If you can remember, think of an emotional occurrence that happened when it first occurred. Using the basic statement as given in **Appendix 2**, add your own words and begin to tap on this situation. This might involve someone else or could be your own response to something that happened.

3. **Positive Habit**

When you get up in the morning what one new positive habit could you introduce into your day that would help you with your life at this present time.

If you are used to having an unhealthy breakfast or a coffee first thing, what could you replace it with for one week?

If you find you achieve this, perhaps you can achieve a second week. It takes 28 days to install a new habit into your programming. You may slip a little after this, but your new awareness will soon direct you back towards it again.

4. **Exercise**

Consider your own exercise regime. Do you do any? If so, is it easy to maintain or is it sporadic? By adding some kind of routine into your life on a daily or every other day basis, will help to ensure that you stick with it. Your body gradually becomes used to it and after a while will remind you when you are lapsing.

Look at some different ideas as to what you would like to do that would make you happy re exercise. You can consider, dancing, running, the gym, pre-recorded exercise routines shown by experts, walking at a fast pace, golfing, badminton, tennis, football, rugby, cycling or anything else you can think of. The main thing is to choose something that can be turned into a daily or every other day routine.

By exercising daily or every other day you will be helping your energy to become revitalized, especially if you can do something outdoors in nature. This is particularly important if your job is a sedentary one (office or home based).

It is easy to fall into the trap of sitting indoors lots, not exercising enough and not getting out into the fresh air.

5. **Diet**

One day a week observe how many portions of fresh fruit and vegetables you are eating.

Eating lots of dead food will cause your energy to become stagnant. When I say dead I am talking about food with no nutritional value and meat. The body takes a long time to process these foods and this can cause you to become sluggish.

By inviting fresh fruit and vegetables into your diet more, it will encourage your body to feel healthier and lighter. One thing that I have observed - if you eat fruit make sure that you have it before a meal or on its own. Fruit ferments inside the stomach when it is eaten. If you eat this after other food it will sit on top of the other foods eaten and cause you flatulence. For me, having learnt the hard way I would rather save myself the embarrassment and discomfort where I can.

Make one day a fruit and vegetable day and see how you feel. If you notice yourself feeling better, add more days into your week and watch as you begin to change the balance of your energy.

The important thing is to have a balanced diet that incorporates all the main nutrients and vitamins that you need for a healthy life.

6. **Mind Map**

Note down one thing that is currently lacking in your life. Using a mind map, draw lines from the centre showing all the thoughts you have been having lately about it. (Mind mapping is a way of focussing the mind onto paper - use the Internet to help you if it is new to you). Observe these thoughts and decide if they are focusing on the lack or the solution. If your focus is on the lack, draw some more lines from these thoughts reframing them towards a solution. If your focus is a solution, great, keep working on this allowing yourself to be drawn towards the answer.

It may be that you simply need to let go of the thoughts about it and trust the universe to give you signs that will help you to achieve it. This is especially the case if no ideas of solutions are coming directly.

7. **Affirmations**

Affirmations are very powerful if used regularly. (See **Appendix 6** for more help with this). Thinking about something that you find difficult about your health, write out an affirmation that is the opposite.

For example:

I find it difficult to give up smoking

Can become

I am happy that I can live without cigarettes

Or

I am smoke free and I love it

At first it will seem a little strange especially if you are still smoking. However, after a while your mind will draw you towards a solution that will help you to live according to the affirmation you have chosen. Trust in the process and it will happen.

Often people give up on their dream just before it is about to happen. There is an example in a story I have come across. Once there was a gold digger who bought land that he knew to be rich in gold. He spent months digging but found nothing. The time came when he decided enough was enough and he sold the land and equipment. Those who bought it did some research and after digging for just one day from the spot where the previous owner had finished they struck gold.

Just one more day and the man would have been rich. Instead someone else benefitted from his dream.

Just because something in your consciousness is not yet visible does not mean it is not there - it simply hasn't reached your awareness yet. Trust and believe in you and the power you have to create and know your life will transform.

Friends

My Story as I saw it then

As a child I found it difficult to make friends, since it seemed that many around me preferred to make fun of me rather than embrace who I was. Being a sensitive child I took what they said personally.

There were a few that warmed to me and I stuck close to them.

As an adult my own challenges with personal love relationships has limited my ability to find stable and reliable friends. There are a few who have stuck with me throughout, loving me no matter what or where I am. For these I am very grateful.

As with my relationships, I have found myself often picking friends who are in need in some way, especially associating with friends who have some kind of depression. Clients have become my friends fulfilling my need to be needed.

At times I have felt disappointed and despondent in the way friends treated me, as I expected and wanted more from the friendship than what was on offer - hence the need to choose friends that had a need from me.

Often I have put friends on pedestals, believing them to be better than me in some way - Comparing my situation to theirs and feeling inadequate in some way.

For example, those who have close families who they see regularly, those who have nice homes and great partners. All of these were reminders of what I lacked in my own life.

If potential friends did come into my life who were wealthy and happy within themselves, I would often withdraw, feeling inadequate and ashamed of my own circumstances.

During this time of spiritual awakening my new friends have tended to be single and in the same place as me, struggling with their finances, unable to find a direction in their life that is fulfilling and learning to walk a more spiritual pathway.

My Story as I see it now

As a child your story is set. If you receive acceptance and love from others you feel encouraged and the best of you is drawn out.

The feeling of rejection by others led me down a pathway of believing less of myself. Although intelligent and very able, my boundary was set at a low target and to rise above it could only happen if encouraged by those around me.

As you may know from your own experience in school, if you are part of the average crowd, you become a number amongst many. Teachers fail to see the true potential in you as they focus on those less and more able. I know this to be true because of the level of qualifications I have achieved since leaving school and during my sixth form when my family moved to a new area.

My individual capabilities were suppressed, along with my emotional self by my reaction to the experiences given to me at school age.

As an adult I have become aware that I could have changed this back then and throughout my life. However, without the awareness that I was creating these limitations or details of how to change, it was not possible until my awareness was focused upon this.

Throwing myself into my marriage, fulltime work and studying for a degree, I had little time for friends. The differences between my husband and I re friendships and life became apparent two years into our marriage. I remember standing on a dance floor at age 22 thinking what have I done. Our needs and desires and sense of adventure being so different. Doing my degree became a great distraction.

When we had children I gained a few friendships, but again these were very limited and as I found out to my peril, not all were good ones.

When I decided to move down South in 2005 with my children, I had in tow a boyfriend with whom there were some challenges. This limited my ability to make news friends easily as my focus was on settling my children into new schools, doing exams for a new career and propping him up.

When we split up the friends I did make were based on adding some fun into my life, which at the time was what I needed.

Moving on to several other love relationships one after the other, friends were very sparse as my time was taken up with developing the new relationships. Looking back I can see that due to the constant unsettlement and unhappiness I was feeling, I had little to offer to friends at the time. Some of those I did have were based on my need to help them and when the help was done they were gone. Only those that had known me a long time that truly cared about me stuck by me.

Once life became a little more settled and I began my spiritual journey, I can see that the friends I attracted were similar to me in order to help show me aspects of myself. Since I had become more aware of my behaviour and me I was able to resonate with them and this allowed friendships to form.

It is true what they say, if you look at your closest friends, you will see a reflection of who you are and where you are at in your own life.

Since I had a low self esteem, had accrued financial debt, was single and lacked direction, many of my friends reflected this to me in some way. It was comfortable being around others who were the same.

Since moving further along my spiritual journey I have begun to attract more sincere and loving friends. As my sense of direction grows new friends are coming into my life who are encouraging and supporting of my visions. Now that I am beginning to believe in who I am, they are too.

It has become clear that in order to succeed in any area of my life, first I must feel successful within myself. Lacking confidence and love for me led me to others who were the same replicating how I felt. To create inspiration and a desire to move beyond this meant a need to change. First I have had to accept and forgive myself for all my journey had been so far and begin to love who I am now and want to be.

Forgiving and loving myself has given me greater clarity. Instead of seeing things through the hurts of the past I can now see the reality as I wish to create it. Within me, I recognise I have the power to change my friendships with my thoughts and feelings and invite those into my life who love, inspire, encourage and support me as I do them. The more I do these things for myself, the more those around me can reflect it back.

By changing the perception I have of me, I can now respond differently to those around, allowing myself to fit in where before I felt I didn't.

That is not to say that I have to conform to be as others are. In fact quite the opposite - now I feel happy embracing my uniqueness because I love and enjoy being me. This means that I no longer need to seek approval from others. It is good to know that those who become my friends now accept me truly for who I am because I have accepted myself.

Although you might feel different from others, believe me it is a blessing. It means that you are aware of your own uniqueness. However, only when you truly love you will you feel comfortable around others for no longer will you seek to fit in. Instead you will simply be happy being you.

For example, my daughter used to ask if something she wore looked nice. My response was as long as you feel good and comfortable wearing it, it does not matter what others think. Be proud to be you.

If you want to wear a purple coat, bright yellow jeans or flowers in your hair, the only person that stops you is you. Other people's opinion of you is none of your business. As long as you are happy and feel comfortable in your choices, you can be whoever you wish to be. There may be consequences to your actions, if say you wear a pair of bright yellow trousers to an interview for a job as salesperson in a posh retail store. However, as long as you are happy to accept these consequences because you are happy being who you are, the world is your oyster. If others can't accept you, it is only their own personal emotional stuff that is responding to you, something you are not responsible for.

This may cause difficulty in some relationships you have especially if their ways are based on rules they have set for themselves or they are fixated on certain ideals. The consequences of being yourself around them may mean you parting company if they cannot see a way to changing their perception.

By being truthful to myself about who I am and who I want to be, I can see that those who are right for me on this journey of discovery will emerge along the way.

By changing my focus to being happy within myself, it allows me to no longer be needy of friendships. Instead I can enjoy those that come my way in the moment they are with me.

Friendships come and go in our lives as we change. We are all here to discover who we are. If who we are changes, it is inevitable that the friends around us will change too. Once we have seen the reflection of our behaviour within them and acknowledged it, they are able to move on or remain if they choose.

Being happy with who I am has invited everything around me to flow with the joy I feel inside. It has given me the ability to appreciate those in my life for who they are and not who I wish them to be. My glass has become half full instead of half empty.

No longer do I see the behaviour of others as rejection. Instead I can appreciate that each person has their own perception of their experiences based on their own unique journey. Their perception often teaches me what I still need to see within myself. This is the beauty of friendship that I have come to love and respect.

Friendships are an opportunity to get to know yourself better and to express yourself in whatever way you wish to be seen, heard and felt. Those that last are based on unconditional love, with no judgment or expectations attached to them.

Tools I have used to help me

Forgiveness

Forgiving others seems to be far easier than forgiving yourself. When you realise that others have merely been playing a part in your life to help you see something within you that needs healing, it is easier to forgive them.

Sometimes the hurt that another causes you is very deep. However, I have realised that it is only my own perception of their behaviour that has created the hurt. Had I been able to stand in **The Safety Zone** and see their behaviour for what it was, I would have been able to send them compassion instead of taking it personally. Having compassion for another's actions is a way of loving them. By seeing that they are simply responding to life based on their own experiences, it helps you to be compassionate towards them. Stepping into **The Safety Zone** allows you to do this.

For example, I once approached a friend quite innocently asking if a new boyfriend of mine (replacing the old one who had been invited) could be my plus one at her wedding if I was to pay for him, as we were to be moving in together. It hadn't occurred to me that I was asking in front of others. To me it seemed an appropriate time and a question that I didn't see any harm in asking. However, my friend saw it completely differently and felt I had embarrassed her in front of her friends into saying yes when she wanted to say no. It resulted in her withdrawing the offer hurting me greatly as I saw it as a personal rejection. However, in that moment I was so emotionally attached to my boyfriend I could see it no other way.

Later I apologised for my reaction when I saw it from her point of view. At a later date she offered for him to join us as someone had pulled out, but by then his pride was hurt and so he found a reason not to come. He did come to the evening do but was disgruntled that I spent most of my time dancing. Shame because it was a beautiful wedding and I am grateful that we were invited.

If I had stepped into **The Safety Zone** and taken the time to calm my emotional self down, things might have been much smoother. Instead emotions created drama and this created upset.

Forgiving yourself for such events means accepting who you were at the time. It means giving yourself compassion, realising that your reactions were based on your own perception of things in that moment.

None of us are perfect. We each have our idiosyncrasies. Being able to accept yourself wholeheartedly and love who you are despite your differences with others, will enable you to flow more easily with life.

When you forgive yourself and become compassionate towards your past, it gives you the opportunity to change your responses in today. This skill also extends to others as you find yourself having compassion for them and their reactions towards you. (See things you can do to help yourself below for an exercise on forgiveness).

Acceptance/Letting go of Rejection

As you learn to have compassion for yourself you will gain more clarity about who you truly are.

You may not like what you see in yourself in this moment because everything within you feels dark and gloomy. However, the more compassion you have the easier it will be to begin to love you.

Expressing compassion for yourself allows you to stop judging you. Instead you will see the person you have become as a result of the experiences you have been through. Accepting this gives you the opportunity to find a new perspective on your life today so that you can begin to respond more positively.

Accepting myself has taken a long time. Others non-acceptance of me was meant as a reflection for me to learn from. Instead it became a series of hurtful experiences until my awareness changed.

By the time you come to a point of acceptance you may have already done a lot of damage to yourself. You may have scars from self harming, you may be over or under weight, you may have piercings all over your body or tattoos that you would never dream of having had you felt good about who you were.

This can make acceptance even harder. However, no matter what you look like at this moment, if you can accept it as simply the result of your journey so far, you can change how you view you now. By seeing each part of you as a reflection of your experiences, it teaches you to see yourself as a piece of art - something that has been created over time using your perception at each moment to guide you.

The creation that you are now may not be able to change physically, but it can change within your mind. You can look at each scar, tattoo, piercing, your body and see the rich tapestry that it is - a collection of memories that have led you to a point of positive change. By having this perception you can learn to celebrate the life you have had and begin to create a new tapestry with a mind that is now for you instead of against you.

To begin with it maybe painful as you let go of hurtful stories you have been holding onto for a long time. However, with each story you let go of there is another opportunity to create a new more positive feeling one. With each new positive feeling story you can begin to create new friendships that are in alignment with the new you that you are becoming.

Gratitude

When you are feeling sad inside, it is very difficult to feel grateful for things or people in your life. Your focus is on the lack and this energy draws your mind to see only what is missing in your life.

Gratitude is a vibration of joy. It helps to open new feelings within that guide you to a life that is happier and more fulfilled.

When I was feeling sad, I felt unsupported and unloved. It didn't matter what anyone did for me at that time, I could only momentarily be thankful - my thoughts reverting back to feelings of sadness after.

If you are not able to feel thankful towards yourself it is very difficult to feel it towards others. This leads you to becoming someone who often gives out a lot to others but very often leaves little opportunity to receive anything back. Some might say this is selfish since you are not giving others the chance to give to you.

By giving to others constantly it is likely you are fulfilling a need within you to feel needed. This may not be consciously in your mind, but within your subconscious mind you have a desire to please others before pleasing yourself. This eventually will lead to burnout or illness as you deplete your energies on others, leaving little for yourself.

Learning to be grateful and appreciate yourself and others means to change your perception. You might be able to say thank you, but do you really feel it inside? Is your heart connected or are they simply words of politeness?

For example, a friend brings you a present. Your mind is on debt and your lack of funds to pay your bills. This present, although lovely, will not solve your problem in this moment. Being able to be truly grateful and appreciative from the heart is likely to be very difficult. You can be polite but your mind is likely to be preoccupied on other things that are dragging your energy down.

Using **The Safety Zone** it can help you to overcome this. By stepping into it and observing your current state of mind, you can redirect your thoughts and feelings to the present moment and give your friend the appreciation they deserve for being so kind. Being present in the moment of now keeps your mind focused on current activities allowing you to be aware of your reactions rather than being disconnected.

As you practice gratitude and appreciation daily the more it will become second nature to you and part of your everyday practice.

Finding things to be grateful for at the beginning and end of a day can help you to focus on what is presently good in your life. Writing these in a journal can be a good way of reminding yourself to do this. You may find that it will also begin to creep into your daily thoughts. The more time you spend on appreciation the greater the joy you will feel in your life.

For example, a friend might send you a compliment via text or email. You might normally find compliments difficult to accept and so always have the need to reply with one back. By stepping into **The Safety Zone** you can release any emotional struggle you feel about yourself in this moment. You can focus entirely on the compliment sent. This will allow you to see their perspective and appreciate their sentiment. As you appreciate it you can accept it and be grateful.

Remember by not allowing others to give you are denying them the gift of giving. Always feeling the need to give a compliment back means reflecting what they have said back to them instead of giving them the chance to be the giver.

Self Love

Self-love is an important part of building new friendships. It allows you the opportunity to love others unconditionally without the desire for them to provide anything in return.

It is unlikely you will receive nothing back as true friends want to give to each other. However, if you find yourself in a friendship where you are the only giver, it is likely that they are reflecting back to you the message to remember to give to yourself.

Friends are mirrors. They reflect back to you your own behaviour to yourself. To have good feeling loving friendships, you first need to feel good and loving towards you.

For example, a friend of mine once asked if I would babysit her daughter whilst she went to the gym, despite knowing my own children were at the child minders whilst I worked from home. My friend was convinced their child would be fine sat in front of the television while I worked. Inside I was upset that she should ask. My answer was no.

Looking back and knowing myself better now I can see that she was merely trying to show me that I did not value my time or myself since normally I was easily persuaded to put others needs in front of my own.

Simple things can mean a lot. It is amazing when I look back how many incidents like this I can see and think, if only I knew then what I know now.

Instead it is simply another opportunity to forgive others and myself and to have acceptance and compassion for what happened then.

Emotional Freedom Technique (EFT)

EFT has been a great tool for helping me to release old negative thoughts and feelings. It has helped me to work through old stories, accepting myself for my part in them and letting go of any feelings of guilt or shame I felt.

Negative memories of times with friends have easily been erased. It has helped to release sad faces sat in my energy giving me the chance to replace them with happy feeling ones.

By removing old responses and feelings it gives me the chance to create new responses.

If you have fallen out with friends over incidents, EFT is a great way to heal the hurt giving you a chance to rekindle your friendship. Whilst you carry the hurt it can be difficult to trust them again. By releasing the negativity around the memory it gives you the opportunity to gain clarity over the reasons for their reflection to you of behaviours you needed to see and experience. Considering your own life and how you treat yourself, perhaps you will see what part they were playing at the time and find forgiveness for what happened.

Everyone in your life is like a player on the stage performing some part alongside you. Every part is important to guide you towards being the best of yourself.

Carrying negative energy around from hurts you have experienced from friends will cause you to feel less inclined to make new friends for the fear you feel of being hurt again.

Ask yourself if friends are important. If so, decide what aspects of your friendships could be better and how you could improve them by being more aware of yourself.

Letting go of Judgment

Whenever you judge another it is yourself you are judging. This is something I have learnt through experience.

Think about it. When you judge someone for their looks, their manners, their way of being, what are you judging it against? The only thing you have to judge against is yourself. Consequently it is not them you are judging but yourself. They are merely bringing up a feeling within you that highlights something about how you feel towards you.

For example, I remember reading a post on Facebook recently about a young girl who has multi coloured hair and tattoos on view. She is a nurse. Many people judge her for the way she looks openly saying to her that she is the wrong job.

She proclaims that her hair and looks do not define her ability to give compassion, to offer kindness, to clean a person or to care for them. They are merely her exterior expression of herself. She is happy with the way she presents herself. Therefore those who judge her are in fact judging themselves as they reveal aspects of him or herself, that they feel are made uncomfortable by her.

Their judgments are likely to be based on previous experiences or social portrayals of nurses and how people expect them to traditionally look. They have nothing to do with the actual ability of the girl.

Times are changing and the way people present themselves is changing with it. This girl's ability to do her job is not affected by the way she looks. In fact it is likely to add some variety to what must be a difficult and challenging place to be for many when they are seriously ill.

Judging yourself keeps your life limited. It fills you with fear of change and closes your mind to new possibilities.

Friends can come in many different forms. If your mind is limited you may be missing out on a friendship that could be the best you have ever had simply because you judged a person by their appearance or some other aspect of them based on your own perception of yourself.

Angels

Angels can help you in any aspect of your life. One of the reasons they are here is to help bring your awareness to the light/love you hold within you and guide you towards sharing it with others.

If friends are lacking in your life, this can be for many reasons. It is likely that you have cocooned yourself away in a safe place of your own so that you no longer have to rely on them for fear of the hurt they may cause.

For example, I had a boyfriend who found it difficult to trust friends because of his challenging upbringing. He had not been shown how to love and so easily became attached to those who showed love towards him. However, if they did anything that showed disrespect for him, no matter what the reason, he found it difficult to forgive them, and often would end the friendship. This kept him safe and his mind right in not trusting anyone. Looking at the situation as I see things now, I can see that it was him he did not trust because of all the hurt that he had encountered along his journey and so could not give that trust to another.

Another example is a gentleman I came across recently. He previously took drugs and drank alcohol. He had been clean for a few years and was finally holding down a job. He worked abnormal hours and so did not have much time in the week to socialise. At the weekends he was simply glad to shut the door of his home and stay cooped up inside until Monday came again. He had been hurt and let down badly by family, friends and love partnerships. He did not want to take any chances on being hurt again and so had become happy with his limited life because to him it felt safe.

As humans, interaction with people is a special part of our lives. Having friends who care for you is a gift and one that comes when you care for yourself.

Working with the angels gives you the opportunity to work through difficult challenges you set yourself with loving support. The angels help lead you to answers that give you a solution to your problem. They will often guide you to people or information that you can resonate with at a point you have the awareness to understand it. Sometimes you might listen and take action from it. Other times your emotional self may be too distracted and prevent you from doing so. Later on the seed that is sown may entice you when you have made changes that make it acceptable.

To invite supportive and loving friends into your life, the angels can help you learn to be supportive and more loving of yourself so that you become more comfortable having such friends around you.

Archangel Raphael can help you to heal any old hurts from past friendships. He is a healer and is always present whenever you call out his name.

Archangel Michael can help to give you the courage to let go of old stories and finally release them. He is a powerful angel and his presence can give you the strength to break free of friendships that are no longer healthy for you.

Accepting help from the angels enhances your own ability to succeed in receiving what you wish for in your life. (See **Appendix 4** - Angels - for more information).

Summary

Friends come into your life often for a reason. Some stay for life, some are only for a short period of time and others simply come to show you something in that moment which is important to help you shift into a higher awareness, creating opportunity for positive change.

The more you accept, love and support yourself the more loving and supportive friendships you will attract.

Lifetime friends are those who you love you unconditionally - warts and all.

Forgiving old hurts between friends can help open the door to new friendships.

Trusting yourself to make the right friendships for you in that moment allows you to accept whomever comes. Not all friends are meant to be long term. Once you have seen what needs to be shared you may simply choose to move on.

Keeping the same group of friends can limit you from meeting new ones that may offer you a deeper and more fulfilling experience. Accepting that as you change your friends will alter too will help you to make positive changes in your life more easily.

Things you can do to help yourself

1. **Forgiveness**

To forgive yourself, you could have a go at the following meditation:

Relax and take 3 deep breaths, close your eyes. Imagine sitting in a darkened room. As you look in front of you, see a light shining on a mirror. Look at yourself in the mirror. See the shadows around you of the past and focus on the light shining upon you. See the beauty of you in the moment of now. Let yourself stand tall and focus upon your heart. Feel your heart opening and allow the energy of love to surround you. The more love you are able to share with yourself, the greater love you will have for others. Watch as the shadows begin to disappear and see those you love dearly standing in the light with you. Feel the love within you growing and glowing from you. When you feel full of love you can open your eyes.

2. **Acceptance**

To find acceptance for you sit down with a piece of paper and a pen. Write out one story that you can remember that has happened to you. Think about each of the characters in the story and how you acted within it. This can be a story where you were the person hurt or where you caused hurt to another.

Write out what part of you feels affected by it. Is it your self-worth, self-love, confidence, self-esteem, self-value, or self-perception?

Consider what this hurtful behaviour was reflecting to you about this aspect of you. Why have you taken it personally? Why is it still playing out in your life?

When you take time to break stories down it helps you to understand them better. The more clarity you gain the easier it is to change the present.

For example, I can remember an incident when one boyfriend flipped into annoyance and anger because I was ten minutes late. He stormed out despite me having warned him on the telephone and explaining fifteen minutes before arriving. At a later date I discovered he was annoyed because he felt disrespected. He felt I had put someone else's feelings before his causing him to feel insignificant in my life in that moment. He explained that the tipping point was me putting another person in front of him when he was already behind my 3 children, making him 5th in line.

It was clear he was used to relationships where he had been number one as his most of his previous partners had no children and so I was able to be compassionate when I heard this explanation.

However, at the time it happened I was mortified by this incident and because it was such an extreme response from him with no explanation I ended the relationship. It was after several months apart that the explanation came when we were once again drawn back together.

Looking back I can see that for him one of the most important things he needed to feel from another was respect. This was based on his stories from the past and the disrespect he felt he had previously suffered. Looking at it from his personal perspective, it would appear to be his own lack of self-respect that enhanced his need to have respect from others. If he had self-respect for himself, there would not be a need to receive it from another.

Without this need for self-respect his rational mind would have seen that ten minutes late with warning was merely someone else's miss judgment of timings and not personal to him. In my perception I was being respectful by calling him. It was his perception that felt it differently based on his own story.

As I have learnt, each experience we undergo goes both ways. From my personal perspective this incident was also to see whether I was willing to show myself personal respect. Was I willing to put myself under pressure to ensure that I would never upset him in the future by not ever being late?

My children will tell you that I didn't learn from this incident, hence why I invited him back into my life for more.

Instead of respecting me I became anxious every time I met with him afraid of the consequences if I was to be late. This was not a good feeling and one I know now was not healthy.

3. **Gratitude and Appreciation**

To change your habits with respect to gratitude/appreciation, find a nice note pad that you enjoy writing in. Every day, spend time thinking of five things friends have said or done for you in your day. See if you can come up with different things daily. Do this over a week and observe how it feels. Take time to look at what you have written at the end of the week. Notice the feeling of gratitude for your friends as you remember all the good things they have done or said that have helped you.

Taking time to appreciate people in your life enhances your love and respect for them. This helps to build stronger friendships.

4. **Judgment**

To let go of judgment first you must become aware that you are doing it.

At the end of a day, think about any person or thing you have judged. It doesn't have to be big. It is likely there will be something you will have judged, even if it is yourself.

Write out the judgment. Now turn it back on

yourself. To understand why you judged the person or thing, look at what it meant to you. Why did you have this feeling or thought?

For example, you may have judged a person for the way they dressed because you would feel uncomfortable expressing yourself outwardly in the same way.

You may have judged someone for their weight because you yourself would find it difficult to look that way. Perhaps you find it difficult to understand how they could allow themself to get to a size that looks uncomfortable to you.

Think about yourself and why this made you feel uncomfortable. Why did you feel the need to have control over someone else's life by judging them for the way they choose to be? It could be that you simply feel a need to help them. Perhaps they do not want your help. This could be seen as controlling behaviour. If it is a child of yours, it may be that being compassionate rather than judgmental is what is needed in order to encourage them to reach out for help from you.

Ask yourself questions until you find the answer and work through the answer to help you eliminate such judgments in the future.

5. **Reflection**

If your friends do not behave towards you as you would like, spend some time writing out the names of the friends you have. Below each name write out the way they are with you. Perhaps you can consider good and bad traits.

Looking at the bad traits, turn them around to you. What is their behaviour towards you reflecting back to you about you and how you are with yourself?

For example, your friend never seems to offer you support when you need it most - they are always there when you feel great but when you are sad, they always seem to be busy.

Looking at yourself based on this, are you supportive of others? Do you always support others before supporting yourself? Do you find it difficult to support yourself and have become needy of others to do it for you? Have you become negative in your approach to life and this negativity has sent friends away that no longer wish to partake in this viewpoint? Do you always focus on the lack of support in your life, therefore creating it?

Once you have your answers you can begin to work through them to identify how you might change your perception to something more positive.

6. **Emotional Freedom Technique**

Using the guide for EFT, think about what statements you could write out that might help you to gain better feeling friendships.

An example might be:

Even though I lack supportive friends, I completely love and accept myself.

Even though my friends never seem to invite me round to theirs, I completely love and accept myself.

Even though my friends always seem too busy to spend time with me I completely love and accept myself.

There will be many you can come up with besides, dependent on how you are currently viewing your friendships.

7. **Angels**

Thinking of something you wish to heal around friendships ask Archangel Raphael to help you:

"Thank you Raphael for helping me to have more supportive and loving friends in my life. "

By saying it as if it is done you are creating it. If you ask as you normally would a request, you are in this moment saying it doesn't exist, and therefore are creating the lack of it. See Law of Attraction above under health for a further explanation on this.

Family

My Story as I saw it then

For me, like many, family is really important. Having such values means I have automatically created expectations based on what I see the role of my family is.

For some reason I seem to have blanked out most of my childhood. There are particularly difficult times I can remember but a lot I cannot. I have been told of some of the traumatic things that happened between my parents during my blank spots and this has helped me to understand myself better. I cannot share the details, as this is private to them. Amongst the memories I have some loving ones of times spent visiting grandparents and Christmas time, which was always special.

I do remember that life was challenging at times. With a strict upbringing and the difficulties faced at school, it felt like there was nowhere that was completely emotionally safe - I had to be careful what I said wherever I went for fear of the consequences.

The day I got married at just 20 years old was the day our family nucleus fell apart. Whilst on my honeymoon my parents told me of their intention to end their 25-year marriage. It felt like any safety blanket that may have been there was ripped away.

My brother moved out of the home and became involved in the pub industry. Sadly this led him down a pathway that was to end in an early death, at just 46.

When my parents split up my mum disappeared out of our lives for one year, the details of which are private to her. My dad found it extremely difficult but like many had to move on with his life. He became close to a lady friend at his work and eventually they became partners. The closeness of their relationship meant that my dad became co-dependent upon her. Sadly, when she died a few years ago her death caused him to suffer greatly and still does today.

Both my parents became distant once separated, each coping with their own challenges. Family gatherings were no longer a possibility except separately. Although childhood had not always been easy, this was still my family. I love them all greatly. To no longer join together felt sad and disappointing.

My husband and his family became my focus. Problems began to show themselves within his family creating difficulty with some members. My different way of viewing and dealing with things meant I was not accepted for a short while by some despite acting in way that I believed to be loving.

Two years after being married I realised I was with someone who was very different to me. Throwing myself into a degree whilst working full time, helped to distract me and provide the fulfilment I needed at the time. I believed in the vows I had taken and felt strongly then that I could make my marriage work.

At 26 I was ready to have my own children and they became my world. Devoting as much time to them as I could, I took jobs that enabled me to be around them whilst I worked. My husband was not happy about this since he would rather I worked fulltime. He found it difficult to give up his independence and would often make comments or take actions that showed we weren't acting together as one unit. This hurt me greatly as my sense of the family unit was strong.

My mum moved away from the Midlands and settled down South as my firstborn turned 1. It felt like she was abandoning us yet again even though in reality the time we spent together was not much different.

A few years later my marriage ended. Two years later I decided to take the children to live down South, about an hour and a half away from my mum. About a year later my ex husband moved to America.

This change left the total care of the children very much in my hands as he only made arrangements to see them once a year.

My brother had a son just before we moved. Due to the nature of my brother's work and our new location it became difficult to see my nephew.

Many times I have broken my heart at the lack of care that my brother seemed to have for my family or me, both before and after the birth of his son. Even when we lived close by he would often invite my parents to personal parties that he had, excluding my family and me. Each time it felt like a rejection.

His inability to connect with his emotions and the development of his new family in the pub meant that he had no need of us in his life. Whenever we visited we were placed at a table in the pub and he would come over and chat momentarily when time allowed.

When his marriage dissolved the new pub he ran created the same scenario. It was only in the last year of his life, due to his illness, that he allowed himself a little more time to spend talking with us, albeit still in the pub whilst he worked. To see us together you would have thought us strangers. We had nothing in common and when I did talk about my life, my brother would often make fun or be sarcastic. Being a sensitive soul this would often upset me greatly.

When he got remarried my heart broke when we arrived at the pub for the reception to find nowhere had been set aside for the family to sit together. We had all driven many miles to be with them. We hardly ever gathered together and yet we were treated as part of his publican family.

When my dad's partner died and my children and I sat in the church, I broke my heart again when one of my children felt we shouldn't be sat in the family bit but should make room for her family. My dad had chosen my brother to sit in the car with him. I felt so alone. My expectations of how family should be totally ripped apart once again.

Since then my father has been in a deep depression finding life hard to manage. When my brother died last year, his grief heightened causing severe anxiety too.

More recently he is beginning to make some sense of his life, but the anxiety and difficulties he feels inside keep his life limited.

My Story as I see it now

The above is a snippet of things that happened to help paint a picture of the disruption and unsettlement that became my normality and how it left me feeling.

Some would say that the biggest disruption came after I left home and so should have been easier to accept. However, despite my great desire to leave home because of the unease there, it had become my normality and I loved my family greatly. To have it taken away with nowhere to run back to if my marriage failed left me feeling alone and abandoned, especially when my mother disappeared for a year.

Looking back now I can see these feelings were my own. My parents acted on their own needs and desires. My reaction to the situation between them was based on my own strong expectation and sense of desire to have a united and happy family unit. I was taking it personally when in fact it was personal to them.

When I consider what I have remembered of my childhood and the bits I have been told, I can see why emotionally I became detached and withdrew inward. Although I still communicated to others, my need to be liked and accepted grew stronger, creating the opposite effect. Since my awakening I have discovered that what we focus on we create. It is clear now therefore that to others my needy thoughts acted like a repellent, making me someone they did not wish to be around.

As children my brother and I were close because friends were very rarely allowed into the house. Once the family unit separated he became distant and his love of alcohol and the party atmosphere meant our worlds grew further apart. This was his own way of dealing with any emotional difficulty he felt.

As my desire for the family to be close grew stronger, the law of attraction ensured that because this was my focus the opposite effect was to occur. My focus on the lack created more lack.

I loved my brother very much. It was hard to deal with the separation that occurred as adults. However, I can see now that we each had our own way of dealing with the circumstances of our family. If I had known then what I know now, I would not have taken his actions personally and felt it as rejection. Instead I would have felt compassion for him and accepted that his journey was personal to him.

It has taught me that each person is responsible for making their own choices for their own reasons. How they respond to others is their own personal reaction to any given situation. It is not a personal attack on another, but instead their way of expressing themselves within the circumstances presented.

Having spoken with colleagues and friends of my brother since his death, I have realised that my brother's way was to be sarcastic and a prankster to others - his way of making them laugh and keeping life jolly. This has shown me even more clearly that my own responses to his sarcasm were based on my personal perception of my own stories created around my brother - stories in my head. His reality was very different. With no connection to his emotional sensitive self due to the effects of alcohol, he was unable to be discerning about his responses to others. His words were therefore meaningless - no malice intended. This was a lethal combination to be on the end of for someone like me who is highly sensitive.

When my parents announced they were parting after 25 years of marriage I was shocked. I had not seen it coming. I am sure my brother was the same.

The differences in my parents' personalities and their own individual needs and desires had grown far apart. Each needed to experience new things that would bring them greater happiness.

No matter what age parents choose to separate, there are always likely to be repercussions to the family unit. Each age of development is affected differently.

Due to my own lack of self-love and low self esteem this separation of the family unit left a big gap in my life. Despite knowing that my marriage was not all I had dreamed of, it was at least somewhere safe to rest my head for a while.

When members of my husband's own family rejected one of his nephews due to his choice of marriage, I found it hard to standby and respond in the same way. It became especially hard when one of his children became seriously ill and so I intervened and helped. Although this difference caused disappointment with the family members involved and a difficulty between us at the time, I can see that I was merely honouring my own truth in helping him.

Today I still standby my actions of offering help. It taught me that to honour your own truth is sometimes difficult especially when others disagree. However, I have also learnt that when your truth is insistent that something feels right to you, it is important to honour it. It is when you don't that you often think back and think if only.

This is an effective way of standing tall and will align you with your power within. When truly aligned you gain an extra strength that before you did not have.

It is good to report that the family members involved do now see their son again and we have once again become friends.

When I had my children, my own sense of creating a close family unit felt disrupted each time my husband sensed his independence being challenged. He resented me working on a Saturday morning, leaving him having to care for his own children. He begrudged giving up his holidays from work to spend time with the family when he had other things he wanted to do. He found it difficult to say he loved me because he was no longer first in line. Attention was now on the children and he felt pushed aside.

Looking back I can see that I married someone who was emotionally distant, like my own family had become, because of his own upbringing. As the youngest sibling by 12 years it must have felt like he was an only child. Suddenly having to share his time with the four of us instead of one must have felt suffocating.

As he relished his own space my husband did not have many friends outside of work. He enjoyed having projects that meant he could be alone, something I can now see he was used to.

Thinking of the Law of Attraction, I can see my need to be loved by him created a sense of lack. My negative focus meant I only saw and felt the negative responses he gave to me. From the tears that came from him when I left him, (I had never seen him cry before), I believe somewhere inside he did love me. I realise now that because we were both emotionally closed, he couldn't communicate it and I couldn't feel it.

As a mum of three small children this behaviour of my husbands felt very isolating and unloving. My journey has taught me that we each have different ways of giving and receiving love.

Our own love language can be seen as follows:

- *Some like to give presents and receive presents*
- *Some like to give time and receive time*

- *Some like to express love through feel and touch*
- *Others like to express love through words.*

If your love language is not the same as your partners, it creates miscommunication and can eventually cause a breakdown between you.

Knowing myself better, I can see my main way of loving is through touch and feel, words and spending time together. Observing my husband with his children over time his main way is to give gifts.

When I look back at my childhood I can see that my way of expressing love was rarely received from my parents due to their own challenges. This was not because they did not love me, but merely that life got in the way. Gifts became the main way that love was expressed, hence why Christmas and birthdays felt special.

Without this understanding back then, this led to me attracting this in my husband and in some of the boyfriends that followed. Now that I can see this I am aware of it and will be less likely to attract someone who loves only in this way. Of course it is lovely to receive gifts and to give gifts. However, if your sense of love is something other than this, no matter how many gifts come, you will always feel a lack of love from them if they do not love you as you like to be loved as well.

When my mum moved down South the abandonment that I felt when my parents marriage had broken came back again. This was my own personal reaction. My mum was simply following a need within her to create a new life and new identity. She changed jobs and settled into a new home.

Even though she had been unable to offer much support to me with my son due to her career, the distance between us meant it was now even more unlikely. Not long after, my father moved up North and so once again the family was torn apart.

However, I can see now that if this had not happened, I may never have believed it possible to move down South myself, something that has been an important part of mine and my children's journey and experience.

When my parents separated across the country, it meant that I was left facing myself. However, instead I spent my time devoted to my three children. I created jobs that allowed me to spend time with them, leaving little time to consider myself.

Just before this a catalyst came into my world that caused me to see how unhappy and unloved I was feeling within my marriage. This was to be the turning point that sent me onto a rollercoaster, leading eventually to change. All the time I kept myself distracted with new relationships and other people's dramas, failing to see who I was or what I had become.

My children were thrown into many different scenarios, each time experiencing extreme emotions. We moved house many times, sometimes with my new partner at that time and other times on our own.

When I look back I am amazed at my children and how well they adapted to each set of new circumstances. My only comfort is to know that this provided a huge learning ground for them that taught them many things about life they could learn no other way.

My children now are doing extremely well in their lives, each of them able to adapt to new environments and changing times as they occur. Despite all the turmoil I put them through, my love and support for them was always strong.

When I had the opportunity I became self-employed, despite high outgoings, using my savings to help supplement things. For me it was important to be at home so that I could encourage and support my children. I was hopeful that a partner would join me in creating a solid family unit.

It was my need to recreate a family unit that kept me on the rollercoaster. It became my obsession. My children just wanted stability and love. I was able to provide this in amongst the turmoil. However, I can see my constant distraction towards each new partner must have been hard on them.

I thank them dearly for hanging in there and riding the rollercoaster with me. Although we have encountered some very difficult times together particularly when tensions ran high, they have come through it as beautiful adults. They are amazing and I love them with all of my heart.

This was not an ideal way to bring up my children. It is clear now I created the same unsettled and disrupted feeling for them that I had rolling around in side of me. If I had been happy with who I was and loved me, I would have settled down much sooner. This lifestyle was so totally opposite to what I wanted for them and yet I could not stop what was happening - I could not see what I was doing. The desire to find love overtook any sense of reasoning when all the time the love was waiting for me inside of myself.

My constant focus on finding the perfect solution for my family meant an even deeper reaction to my brother's behaviour, leaving me feeling rejected and saddened each time I saw him. Now I know the full facts about my brother since his death, I can see that his safety was in the family he had created within the pub. His ability to make them all laugh becoming an important distraction for himself away from his own self. Other people became more important and his own health suffered as a result.

It is easy now to see that he too couldn't stop it. He was on a rollercoaster just like me, except his was a different kind.

As I changed my life and became more aware of whom I was, the gap grew bigger between my brother and me. It simply gave him more ammunition for his sarcasm.

It was only my own need to feel love from him that created my reaction of taking what he said to heart. To him they were just words, his normal way of being jovial. To me they were rejection. As I said earlier my reaction to them was based on my own personal perception of the situation and my sensitive nature.

The same can be said of my dad. His way of dealing with difficult things in life is to go into depression. Once in this state he is unreachable. He is safeguarding his own emotions by suppressing them. His way of protecting himself felt painful in the past. As I see it now, it was my own need and expectations of what I wanted from my dad that caused me to feel hurt.

My mum also locked down her emotions during their marriage, and after, making her unreachable too. The same expectations and need that I had projected onto her as my mother meant that I also felt hurt and disappointment when she did not fulfil them - even more so because she was my mother. These feelings were based on my own interpretation of the experience I was receiving. This left me with no one in the family I could turn to for emotional support.

It was these experiences along with the string of failed relationships that led to me finally finding emotional support within myself. Without them I would never have realised this was possible and so I say thank you to my family and boyfriends for the inspiration and experiences they have given to me.

Now I accept that I am responsible for the way I feel. That no one else has control of this. By allowing others to have control of my emotions means that I am not standing tall in my own power. Instead I am giving my power away and allowing myself to be weakened by others. It is not their intention to weaken me but the stories I create in my head that cause the feelings and emotional response.

Now I can honestly say that by understanding my experiences better it has taught me to love more deeply. It has enabled me to appreciate and love my family for the individuals they are rather than through the expectations I had of them. It has allowed me to release judgments of others and myself. It has given me the confidence to love unconditionally more than was ever possible before.

Tools I have used to help me

Letting go of Expectations

One of the greatest gifts I have learnt from my journey so far is to let go of expectations.

Expectations are based on the past or an ideal of how you would like something to be.

When expectations are not met they can cause tremendous disappointment, especially if this is all you focus upon.

For example, my expectations of wanting to bring my parents and brother together for my Dad's birthday in December 2015 meant that I felt disappointed when it did not happen. In my mind I was hoping my brother would feel the same way given how sad my dad had been. However, he did not or could not come. My mum also decided it would be too much for her because of Christmas being so close.

The sadness that this did not happen was heightened when my brother died in April 2016. However, we did all manage to see my brother together just before he died around his hospital bed so what I focused on did come true, just not how I had expected.

A lot of problems that happen in families are the result of expectations - parents expecting their children to behave and to respond to them in certain ways - children having expectations based upon the expectations taught.

When these expectations are not met, it is often taken personally and hurtful comments and behaviour can result.

For example, a parent is brought up with good table manners. They have expectations that their children will be the same. When a child constantly refuses to be controlled by these rules, the parent becomes upset and often sees it as disrespectful to them. It may simply be that the child prefers to be more relaxed when eating, or maybe they have a blocked nose and are finding it difficult to close their mouth. Whatever the reason, it is the fact that it is taken personally by the parent that causes their reaction - often a negative one.

A young child below age 13 who is sensitive might find it difficult when their parent constantly criticizes their work. The expectation from a child when they bring work home to a parent is to feel loved by the encouragement they hope to receive. When a parent offers criticism, they do it based on their own perception - perhaps due to their own high expectations or because they believe they are encouraging the child to do better next time. However, this can often have a negative effect on the child.

The child takes what is said personally and begins to believe that they are not good enough. That their work is inadequate. They do not have the cognitive skills at a young age to see it as anything other than disappointment from their parent. Disappointment also creates a sense of not feeling loved.

By showing encouragement to a child it creates a loving feeling. It gives them the safety to express themselves freely. This is extremely important at this stage of development if a child is to grow up confident and happy.

By letting go of expectations it is important also to let go of judgment for the judging of a person and situation is based upon an expectation.

Letting go of Judgment

One day I had an epiphany. It dawned on me that I had been judging my parents and my brother based on my own needs and expectations.

They were each simply being themselves when interacting with me. My reality of how I expected them to be was distorting my vision of them.

This distortion on my vision led me to feel great disappointment. This disappointment meant that I did not always get the best out of my relationship with them.

Each time that I created something based on a judgment of how I wanted something to be, it led me to an emotional response of hurt. It felt like they were deliberately acting that way in order to hurt me. Now I can see that no one can hurt me. They were simply acting that way based on their own view of the world. My response was entirely my own.

By learning to let go of judgment I am now able to see each person individually for who they are. However, to do this first I had to let go of my story.

Letting go of my Story/Self Awareness

The stories from my past remain in my past. Today is a new day. Their imprint however, is clearly shown in my current responses to the world and those around me.

To truly change what has happened so that I can create a different life, it became apparent that first I needed to let go of the stories and stop living within the boundaries of them.

Each time I repeated out loud or in my mind something negative that happened to me, my body became saddened and my mind clouded with shadow. This affected how I was in each day.

Each story that has formed my life so far has been a play for me to interact in. I have played my part and the other actor/actresses theirs. We have each taken what we needed from the experience and our lives have moved on.

The difficulty for many people, especially when those experiences have been traumatic, is the damage to the mind from the experiences they have had. Thinking back to the scenario that we are each computers being programmed daily, when a virus takes hold, it can mess up many parts of the computer system, in some cases causing it to burnout completely.

This burnout happens to those particularly who are unaware of the virus. The more aware you are of yourself the easier it is to stop such viruses/stories causing mass destruction. Becoming self aware and present in your daily activities really can make a huge difference to your life. **The Safety Zone** enables you to prevent these viruses/stories getting out of control.

The reality is that once an event has happened it is gone. Like watching a film on the television. Once it is over it is time to move on to the next event.

However, the vibrations of an event or film still remain for quite some time afterwards. If you are not aware of any negative energy collected as a result, it will stay with you embedding itself into your core. If left unattended, each time something similar occurs it will rise to the surface to remind you it is there. After several attempts of showing itself, it will eventually become an illness or pain in the body to ensure you take notice of it. Think of it like the two-year-old child within you having a tantrum because you are not listening to it.

EFT is a great way of releasing the emotional attachment of a story. This allows the memory of it to remain but any negative response to go.

By letting go of each story that has a negative impact on your life, you can leave space for new more positive ones to form. The greater your awareness the happier the two-year-old within you will become as you listen more to them.

Emotional Freedom Technique (EFT)

EFT is free to use and can have a huge positive impact on your life.

Memories that are unpleasant of situations that have caused you hurt will often create difficult and challenging results in future events.

EFT has given me the opportunity to change all aspects of my life and is helping me to create a better future as a result.

When using **The Safety Zone**, you can begin to deal with issues in the moment as they arise. This allows you to create a new response immediately, changing the effect of what has always been before. This is particularly useful around family matters and members since they are in your life the longest.

For example, imagine a family member says something to you that feels negative, maybe an attack on your character in some way. If you were able to go into another room, stand in **The Safety Zone**, and whilst in the orange zone, use EFT to clear the negative emotional feeling, it would allow you to see the reality of what is being said and come up with a rational response.

The words that another is saying are merely their own perception based on how they see the world. For example you may be wishing to change careers and are doing everything you can to set up your own business. Your family may see you as failing because you are not earning the income you did before or they think you capable of because you are relying on benefits to supplement you. Their perception is based on their own need for security. If they have only ever been employed they cannot possibly understand the desire to be self-employed from your perspective.

They do not share your vision and feel the passion you have. They can only see things based on their own experience. Their own feelings of shame around benefits can also have an impact on their words.

Once you can see this you can tap using EFT to remove any feelings of rejection. By standing tall you are allowing your own power to shine giving you the confidence and courage to stand by your own convictions and no longer be offended by others.

There are many scenarios that EFT can help you create better outcomes for. By being aware of it and using it when needed, it will soon become like your best friend, something you appreciate greatly.

Inner Child

As a child you are vulnerable and all that you experience becomes the stage from which you create your future. If you have experienced hurt as a child, it is likely that what you experience as an adult will bring these hurts back to the surface.

Working with your inner child can be very powerful when learning to heal these old hurts. Learning to love your inner child as the parent you are now will encourage them to heal and enable you to stand by their side as they change their responses.

As the hurt child within you changes their responses, you as the adult will change too. You will begin to see experiences from an adult point of view rather than from the emotion of a child.

Your family may not have been loving or kind during your upbringing but as you have grown you will have witnessed this loving behaviour in others. Watching how others achieve this can inspire you to teach your child within to do the same. As you undo the past hurtful experiences you can begin to trust yourself. As you trust yourself it will give you the courage to trust others as your mind lets go of the fear of being hurt.

As you attract better feeling experiences into your life, your response to your family will change and as a result their reaction to you is likely to as well. If it does not, how you perceive them will be different and this will enable you to give them compassion instead of reacting from a personal point of view - from emotional hurt, enabling you to love them as they are.

Forgiveness

Forgiving others is hard if you have not yet forgiven yourself.

By learning to forgive yourself you are experiencing what it feels like to forgive. Only then can you know how to express it to others.

When I realised it was me who had been creating all the scenarios in my life that caused me hurt, it was hard to forgive such ignorance. If I had known what I know now, my life and that of my children could have been saved a lot of the heartache and challenges that we have faced.

However, I cannot change the past and who I was then. It is not possible to go back in time and change the data on my computer that was running at that time. The only time I can make any difference to is NOW.

As a child we are taught so much at school and yet the most fundamental thing, that of how to cope with life, is taught by those around us based on their own experiences. If those around us have faced difficult challenges and been discouraged as children themselves, often they have no way of seeing how to do things differently with us as their children unless someone or something else shows them. This is why negative patterns are often repeated within families.

Sometimes if abuse is encountered, it can create an extreme opposite reaction causing parents to become overprotective of their own children because of the fear that has built up within them.

When I have been unable to forget and forgive certain behaviours of family members, it has distorted my relationship with them. It has created an expectation to receive more of the same instead of being present in the moment of being with them. According to the Law of Attraction, I was simply creating more of the same because what happened was my focus and belief. If I had forgiven, I would have been more willing to be open to them behaving differently and would not have taken their actions and words personally.

For example, my brother would often be sarcastic about my choice to become vegetarian. A boyfriend of mine, who was also vegetarian, found this to be disrespectful and hurtful. Having forgiveness for my brothers' insensitivity now enables me to understand him better. It was simply his way of being. He meant no malice. He simply found pleasure in making jokes out of anything he could, even if others didn't appreciate them. He had no way of being discerning and connecting to other people's sensitivity since he was emotionally desensitised by his lifestyle choices.

It was only possible to change my previous hurtful perception of his comments by forgiving the past and replacing the hurt for compassion. By taking the time to understand a person better it is easier to accept them for who they are. It allows you to let go of your expectations of them based on your own needs.

This is letting go of control. (See relationships for more about this).

Gratitude/Appreciation

When my mind was filled with negative thoughts about the behaviour of my family towards me, based on previous experiences with them, it was difficult to feel appreciation towards them.

Only when I learnt to appreciate myself and forgive me for my way of seeing things, was it possible to begin to appreciate them.

Loving and appreciating yourself helps draw your mind to positive thoughts. This new way of seeing things automatically teaches your mind to see the positive in others too.

By seeing my parents and brother as individuals rather than trying to fit them into a stereotype based on my expectations of how I felt they should be, has released all previous boundaries set. It is possible now for me to appreciate the little things they do, or did in the case of my brother, which has deepened my love for them as a result.

This experience has shown me that appreciation is a way of expressing and feeling love. By being grateful for things, it means to feel joy. Joy is a feeling that comes from the heart and is therefore love.

The more connected you can become to your heart and let go of the mind, the easier it is to love all, to forgive, to let go of expectations and judgment and to finally appreciate all that is in your life rather than focusing on the lack.

The more you appreciate things and people you will find it coming back to you. This has been particularly noticeable with my children. The more I have appreciated and loved them because I have connected with my heart, the more they appreciate and are able to show their love back.

Summary

You are born into your family to experience aspects of yourself that you would never experience in any other way. How you respond to these experiences defines the future you create.

Learning to let go of hurtful thoughts and feelings by forgiving others and yourself will help to release negative energy within you. It will change your responses to those who you feel hurt you and give you the ability to feel compassion and love for them instead.

Appreciating your family and the lessons they have shown you can be a step towards forgiveness if forgiving them is too difficult. Seeing the higher perspective of what you have learnt about yourself from the experiences given can alter your perception.

Taking things personally often means that you are placing some kind of judgment or expectation on another - their actions or comments consequently disappointing you as your judgment or expectation is not met. Learning to see through your judgments and expectations and letting them go, will automatically release any tensions between you and allow you to see each family member and accept them for who they are rather than who you wish they were.

Things you can do to help yourself

So many families have become disjointed because of hurtful things that have been said and done. You may recognise this in your own family. Below I have given some ideas that you can consider that might help you to unlock the past and to create a healthier future with your family.

1. **Expectations and Judgments**

Write a list of those closest to you in your family. Write below each one, your opinion of them. Be honest, this is only for you to see.

Taking each person in turn consider what you have written about them. Decide which parts are based on expectations and which are judgments. Look for what needs to be forgiven.

2. **Consider yourself**

Now write out a passage about yourself. Be honest about how you feel about you. Taking this information, look for all judgments and expectations you have of you. Consider what needs to be forgiven.

3. **Forgiveness**

Compare both tasks and see what repeats itself. It is likely that you will see similarities in how you view yourself in the views you have of your family.

If you accept that your view of yourself and your family has been distorted based on your expectations and judgments do the following forgiveness task:

Thinking of the people you wish to forgive, which can include yourself, find a room where there will be no interruptions. Sit somewhere comfortable and close your eyes.

Imagine yourself sitting in a chair in front of you. If you like you can make this chair the same colour as you would see yourself in this moment. When you feel connected to you, say the following:

"I forgive you and I release you with love. I hold no un-forgiveness back. My forgiveness for you is total. I am free and you are free." (You could add "I love you" at the end if you feel you can to strengthen what you have said).

Imagine the colour of the chair changing to green as you say the words. This is a healing colour. If your chair started as green, you can always change the colour here to something else so that a signal will go to your mind that change has happened.

Now imagine each person on your list sitting before you, one at a time and repeat the process for all.

4. **Appreciation**

Write out the names of each person again, including yourself. Now write out all the things you appreciate about each of them and are grateful for.

If you see these people regularly, especially yourself, do this list every day for one week. Notice all the things you are managing to find that are beginning to change your perception of them or you.

5. **Emotional Freedom Technique**

If you find you are not ready to forgive or let go of judgment, you can use EFT to help.

Write out a statement, based on the notes in **Appendix 2**, about how you feel. For example:

Even though I cannot forgive (Place a name here) I completely love and accept myself.

Even though it is hard to let go of all negative judgments of (place a name in here) I completely love and accept myself.

When doing this tapping, you may find that the reasons behind why you cannot forgive or forget show themselves. Write these reasons out as statements and again tap using them. Eventually you will notice yourself changing towards this person and begin to feel love that before you had been blocking.

For example, you may have lived with a parent who was an alcoholic. Your other parent could have been too fearful to protect you and consequently you may have been physically or verbally hurt on occasion as a result.

Your view of the other parent that you thought should have protected you could be very low. You may see them as weak and find it hard to forgive them.

Using EFT you can work on forgiving both of your parents, the abuser and the one you felt didn't protect you.

Statements might include:

Even though my (parent) was/is an alcoholic, I completely love and accept myself.

Even though my (parent) had/has no control over their actions when they were/are drunk, I completely love and accept myself.

Even though my (parent) was/is unable to protect me because of their own fear, I completely love and accept myself.

As you accept yourself you can learn to view each parent as individuals. You can begin to understand that something in their own lives was creating this response within them and it was not personal to you. It will help eliminate the sting of the emotion from the story and recreate it as simply a memory of something that happened.

It may be that your parent rejected you when you were born. This can be very hard to overcome. However, by using EFT you can begin to see the story clearer.

Instead of seeing what you expect of them, you will see how they may have seen things based on their own experience. It was not personal to you but instead personal to them. They did not reject you because they wanted to be cruel. It is more likely it would have been because of their mind-set and how they felt about life in that moment.

It would have been based on their circumstances and how others viewed them. If they had been raped it could be that you were simply a reminder of the awful thing that happened to them. It was their own personal view and nothing actually to do with you.

When you can clearly see this and be accepting of it, it allows you to forgive and forget so that you can begin to express love and compassion to them. They may not be able to receive it because of their own guilt or fears of being rejected. However, the more accepting you are of your parents, the less anything they say or do will have any impact on you. The less you respond negatively, the dynamics of the relationship will naturally change.

Also looking at The Law of Attraction, because your focus has changed from the negative and is now able to see them through compassion, what you will create will be a new and different relationship. If their behaviour continues because they are too emotionally disconnected to feel any change, it may mean that you lessen the times you have contact, or because you are standing tall in your truth, you may now have the courage to speak to them about it.

Seeing that you have changed may be the encouragement they need to change themselves. Trust yourself to let go of any expectations of what will happen and know that all is perfect as it is.

Wanting them to change is a need to control another. Everyone is unique and entitled to experience the world in whatever way they wish. If holding onto the past is their choice, there is nothing you can do to change it except be in acceptance of it and love them unconditionally if you feel you can.

Each person has the free will to choose if they wish to change. It is for them to see or want the benefits in order to be incentivized. Only when people hit rock bottom do they often accept change is the only way they can survive another day.

Death

My Story as I saw it then

Death is a subject that many find difficult because it is a reminder of our own mortality and often the painful loss of someone close.

My first memory of death that had any real impact on me was the murder of a school friend on her way home one evening. She was just 15.

Although we were not close friends, perhaps more acquaintances, her death was a shock to us all. It was a reminder that life could be extinguished from us without any notice.

The second death I can recall was that of a dear distant cousin, born within 4 weeks of my youngest daughters birthday. He was just 4 when he passed away. It was so sad to think of such a small child experiencing so little of the world.

As a family we experienced the death of pets such as hamsters and fish, like many other people, between then and my grandparents passing gradually one by one when in my 30s.

Although I loved my grandparents dearly, their loss was acceptable because each had reached a good age in their lives.

As each grandparent died I encouraged my children to come along to the funerals, since I felt it was important for them to see death as a normal part of life. There was only one to which they were refused because of my grandfathers views of children at funerals at the time.

The first experience of trauma felt by death came via our cat Thomas. He was 20 years old and near the end of his life. He had moved around many times with us and was very much a part of the family.

One day out of the blue the RSPCA turned up on our doorstep. The man had been told of a cat that looked emaciated around the area and had come to investigate. Explaining how old Thomas was I showed him his bed and food etc. The man advised me to take him to the vets for a check-up, other than that he could see he was happy.

The vet said he hadn't got long left but he was not ready to go and so he came home. On Friday 1st April, just days later, I let Thomas out. We lived in a quiet cul-de-sac. I had tried to block the gate, but he squeezed through. A while later I suddenly wondered where he was. Frantically I searched for him outside knowing he never ventured far from home. After a while I knocked on a neighbours door to see if they had seen him. They said they had and given him to another neighbour earlier thinking him to be theirs.

It was relief I felt as I knocked on their door, until the man answered. He proceeded to tell me they had taken Thomas to the local vets who had put him to sleep. The neighbour said he thought he was a stray!!

Based on the evidence of Monday, the fact that his wife could not face me and never has and having found out the RSPCA had been called on these neighbours about their dogs several times, I have to say I now doubt that.

However, in this moment my heart broke. I was devastated. I lost control of my emotions and wept for hours. The next day I went to visit him, having been advised where he was by the neighbour. Thomas looked peaceful curled up in a ball. As we were in rented accommodation, I didn't wish to bury him and agreed for him to be cremated.

A few years later I experienced yet another traumatic death with my other cat Lupa. He was just 6 years old. He became ill suddenly in the night. During the night his breathing was rattling and he kept crying out. I sang to him and did my best to help him be comfortable, intending to take him to the vets in the morning. I asked for help from the angels. He had a sore back and so I believed between that and a possible cold coming on he would be cured. At 5am in the morning his back legs went from under him and he fell down the stairs. Only then did I realise how serious it was. I took him to the emergency vets service. The problem was a clot on his lung and in his body. They said the only answer was to put him to sleep.

This broke my heart, as I loved him so deeply. We all did. To watch a life instantly disappear was devastating, especially when I was the one who made the final decision. This sent me into shock and I found it difficult to get over emotionally. My expectations of him being so young compared to my other cat, made it seem impossible in my mind that it could be his time.

My brother had been seriously ill in hospital about 1 month before. He too had had problems with his lungs and they had drained them for him. When Lupa died, I could not understand why the vet had no way of doing the same. It seemed to me at this point that human life is treated very differently from that of animals. This was a difficult realisation to come into my awareness.

A year later my brother was rushed to hospital. He had serious problems relating to Pancreatitis which were death threatening. Given the experiences of the previous year, when he was admitted before, I felt it ok to leave visiting to the Wednesday.

When I arrived on Wednesday I was intending only on staying briefly, expecting to drive up and collect my dad from Norfolk to come back Thursday.

However, my brother was like a rabbit in headlights when I arrived. He had begun to seriously deteriorate. My dad was called and had to drive himself down, which he did, despite being highly anxious.

As I sat down in the waiting room with my mum and his wife the angels told me that my brother was going to die. Supporting my family as best I could through the night we took it in turns to be by his bedside. I didn't mention what I had been told. I simply acted with hope like everyone else and asked for healing to be given that was in line with Stuart's higher self's wishes.

In the morning my brother was admitted to surgery and he had a major operation. He survived and everyone sighed with relief, since we had been warned it was touch and go.

Later that afternoon my brother came to and we were allowed to see him, despite having been told he would be kept asleep for at least 24 hours. When he first saw us he said he thought he had died and gone to heaven. He was very confused.

He made it steadily through the night and the next day we all spent time being by his side, chatting to him. Although in a lot of pain he seemed to be doing well.

We were told his recovery could take two months in hospital and so I made a decision to go home and come back another day. This allowed my dad to feel comfortable with doing the same. At this point I was beginning to doubt the message I had received from the angels.

An hour later I stopped to see a good friend before driving back down South. As I was having dinner, my mum called to say my brother had been taken back into theatre. I knew then in my heart the angels were right. This was going to be it.

Driving back to the hospital I sensed he had already gone. When I arrived it was confirmed.

Seeing my brother lying there, empty, was a strange experience. No sign of the character I knew. Only a body to show for the life he had lived.

The funeral was like that of a celebrity, so many joining it that had come to know him over the years through the two pubs he had run. To make the funeral possible between them they had raised over £8,000, since he had nothing of his own to pay for it.

My parents understandably found it difficult to accept that their son had died before them. My father was transported back to the death of his partner just 2 years before. Neither could connect with me at the funeral. Although supported by my children at my side, I felt the distance between my parents and me.

My Story as I see it now

Looking back over the experiences I have had of death it has taught me that life is precious indeed. Each day that we have to live upon the Earth is a gift - an opportunity to express ourselves and to find joy in what we see and do.

When the girl at school died, it felt strange. Murder was something you read about in the papers or today see in films. It seems incomprehensible that someone so close could be taken from us in this way.

Life can be cruel sometimes it would appear, although based on my learning since my spiritual awakening, I have gained an understanding that not everything is as it seems.

My new perception is that each of us is part of one consciousness experiencing different levels of emotion for the greater good of all. Each person that undergoes such horrific experiences has a story to share with others, some of whom have endured the same. Each experience that is shared offers gifts to others to help them experience less pain and suffering than those before.

As each experience teaches new ways to cope, it brings with it the opportunity for the world to change. Many have been asking for a more loving world. For this to happen, first behaviour that is not loving must be revealed. Since the feelings of death are often based around fear and attachment, experiences of this must first be shown before true unconditional love can be felt.

Each time that I have felt trauma and pain from a death it has been the result of my attachment to that animal or person.

Through my spiritual work I have learnt that attachment is not unconditional love. It is instead a need to fulfil the desire for love or affection. This need becomes painful when revealed once more as a person or animal dies.

Learning to love the self gives an opportunity to experience animals and people in your life as a gift for the time they are with you rather than being attached to them. As they die, loving with no attachment makes it easier to celebrate all the magical times you shared and to forgive all that was not meant to be carried for life.

When I have broken my heart over death, it has been my own sense of loss that created it. The animal or person that died is now at peace. In my understanding they have moved on to a far greater and happier place than the earth. They are no longer in solid form and so their spirit is now pain free. Their spirit is now surrounded by the loving thoughts of others who have moved back into the consciousness.

It is only when we step out of the consciousness of love and into the mind, that negative feeling thoughts and actions take place. The consciousness that is the universe is nothing but love. The free will that human beings have is their ego, which is based in the mind. This ego creates feelings and thoughts based on fear.

When we become aware of our ego - the thoughts in our mind that are not coming from love - it reveals to us aspects of ourselves that need to be healed. Once healed, these thoughts no longer come and loving ones are able to prevail.

Death for many is a mystery. It seems unquantifiable unless some proof of what happens is given. Yet even with substantial amounts of proof expressed in many different ways and mediums upon the earth, there is still much doubt as to what the truth is.

We can therefore only ever see the world through our own eyes. What resonates with one person may not resonate with another. Those who can make no sense of another simply perceive their experiences in a different way at the time their views collide.

When I share my beliefs with my children or those close to me, I have understood not to take it personally when they express an opposite view. It does not make either of us right or wrong. We are simply experiencing the world in our own unique way.

It is this unique approach that gives opportunity to everyone to investigate their own truth and express it as they see it. Each new way that is viewed alters the consciousness as a whole.

If the majority of thoughts in the consciousness are dark and negative, the world receives experiences to match this revealing that which is light. If the thoughts are light, the world receives pleasant and loving experiences revealing that which is dark.

Each of us therefore experiences death differently based on our perception of what we believe happens when we die and the experiences we have shared with the person or animal whilst they were with us.

When I have spent time watching and being in nature it has shown me that nothing in life is permanent. Every day that we wake a part of nature has grown and another part has died. Nothing ever remains the same.

As parents losing a child, no one can ever imagine what this feels like unless they have experienced the same. Therefore I could only express compassion to my parents when my brother died. My only ability to empathize in that moment was to know what it is like to have a miscarriage.

My parent's sense of loss was of course much greater and therefore far more painful. For my father, my brothers' death has been a reminder of all the pain he is still suffering from the loss of his partner. For my mother it has been a shock. The effect of losing a child that she gave birth to and nurtured to adulthood.

Observing how each of us has responded to his death, including my brothers' first and second wives and his son, has shown me that for each of us death is a personal journey. When someone dies it reveals to us the things we wished we had said, the times that were treasured, the challenges we had together, loving moments shared, anger and frustration that they didn't take care of themselves.

All of the difficulties that I felt with my brother simply melted away at the moment of death, no longer a reason to hold on to them. All that had happened was gone and no longer relevant. It was all simply stories in my head.

It helped me to see the madness that we carry around with us in our minds that we create our lives from. If I had been able to let go of the stories during his life and see his character as personal to him, I would have experienced a different and more loving relationship with him.

Despite our differences, I have always and will always love my brother. His gift of teaching me not to take words said to heart and to stand tall in my own convictions will live with me forever. Using **The Safety Zone**, I now have a tool that enables me to see when I am taking things said personally.

He enjoyed his life often taking risks to his health. He may not have been quite so willing had he known the outcome. However, everything we do, say and think has consequences. Death just happens to be one of them.

When I look back on the death of Thomas, my beautiful 20-year-old cat, I can see that divine intervention took place. The neighbours thought they were doing the right thing for him and so now I feel only compassion for them. They had their own lesson to learn from it when they saw the devastation of their actions in my face and eyes.

At the time I was distracted with many things and was unable to face the thought of Thomas dying. The decision was taken from my hands.

When I look back at Lupa dying, I see that the effects of what happened to Thomas and my denial that he could possibly be seriously ill at just 6 stopped me calling the vet earlier. Had I done so the decision to put him to sleep would have been harder as it was only when his legs went that I saw the seriousness of it and the true suffering that he was in. It broke my heart to let him go. I can see now why perhaps the same decision had been denied me with Thomas.

Sometimes if we love another unconditionally we have to do what is right for them. Lupas' fate lay in my hands. I could have held on to him for a few more hours, but it was obvious the pain and suffering he was in was already great. All I could do was trust in the words of the vet. After all they are the experts.

Tools I have used to help me

Meditation/Mindfulness

When my mind has been filled with emotion meditation has helped me to bring peace and harmony to it. By becoming aware of my emotional thoughts I have been able to bring to the surface what needed to be healed.

All experiences create some kind of response within us. When someone or an animal dies, we are reminded of our own mortality. Added to this the attachment we have to that person or animal, any unhealed hurts that are still held within, the age they are dying are all factors that affect our emotional response to the situation.

What I have realised through meditation, is that often the thoughts that come around death are based on my own sense of loss, any guilt I feel, disappointment at the way things could have been, memories of the past etc.

Meditation/mindfulness is a way of bringing my mind back to the reality of now. All of the thoughts I had around death and losing a person or animal did not change the reality that the animal or person was gone. Instead they caused me to continue to feel hurt and upset.

It made me realise that by focusing on the good times with them it would be easier to let them go. Carrying such memories creates positive feeling thoughts around their death enabling love to blossom and fear and negativity to fade.

Meditation can be used to help you let go of the attachment to a person or animal's energy so that you and they can move on. You could try imagining the person or animal sat next to you in a meditation. Speak to them and let them know how you feel about them. You can chat for as long as you like. When you feel ready, give them a big hug and watch as they leave the room closing the door behind them. Surround the door in yellow as they go, leaving you with a sunshine feeling of love and warmth whenever you think of them. If you don't feel ready when in the meditation, simply say goodbye and watch them move somewhere else in the house. When you are ready add the extra bit of the door and the colour yellow. (See **Releasing and letting go** below for more information on attachments).

Emotional Freedom Technique (EFT)

Experiencing another dying will more often than not bring with it some kind of emotional response. EFT is one of the best tools to help release the negative effects of the emotions to the body.

When I think back to Thomas and Lupa dying, both caused an element of shock. I wasn't prepared for either. Consequently I was left feeling broken hearted by their departure.

When I remember my brother dying, I see that the time given by the angels to me to adjust to the idea that he might die, helped my mind prepare for what was about to happen. When he looked like he was recovering, it felt like we had hope. It made me think that perhaps all the healing prayers that were being sent by his friends were having some impact. The finality of him dying a day later caused a great sadness to surge in at the moment of hearing the news - the realisation that what I had heard had become a reality. The prayers had eased his suffering but not in the way people had hoped.

Nothing can prepare you for the loss of a person or animal that is close to you. Only when you experience it do you truly know how you feel. If illness is long and drawn out, the desire to let them go because of their suffering, helps give a reason for their death. This can help ease the grieving process.

When someone is murdered or killed in an accident the shock of not being able to say goodbye can enter the body deeply. EFT can be used to help clear the trauma without having to relive it, although it will bring up the sadness for that is what it is designed to do so that it can be released.

Statements that you might use around death might be:

- *Even though (name) has died I completely love and accept myself*
- *Even though we did not get time to say goodbye to (name) I completely love and accept myself*
- *Even though I was not prepared for the death of (name) I completely love and accept myself*

- *Even though I miss (name) greatly and find it difficult to let them go I completely love and accept myself*

Forgiveness

Your experience of death with that person or animal will form part of the relationship you had with them.

My experiences each had some level of forgiveness that needed to be addressed before I could move on from the hurt. Sometimes this can be years later. If you still become emotional when talking about a lost loved one, it is likely there is still some element of healing that needs to be done.

Negative feeling emotions are the biggest indicator to you that you are still holding on to past hurts.

With regards to forgiveness, when Thomas died I had to forgive myself for not opening the door sooner to find him. If I had thought about him earlier instead of being busy with my accounts, I would have found him before the neighbours did and could have made the decision myself to take him to the vet.

When Lupa died I had to forgive myself for not realising how seriously ill he was. There is nothing the vet could have done for it was his lungs that had gone first, but could they is the question that goes through my mind. However, I realise it would have been much harder to make the decision to let him go without seeing his back legs fail.

When my brother died I had to forgive myself for taking things personally that he had said, distorting the relationship we had. I also had to forgive him for not taking care of himself and leaving a 12-year-old son behind.

To forgive does not mean to forget. Instead it means to let go of the pain and suffering you encounter each time you bring the negative thoughts to your mind.

Releasing and Letting Go

One of the hardest parts of experiencing death is releasing and letting them go.

If you are not able to accept that they died and the way they died, this can be particularly hard.

What I have learnt as part of my spiritual journey is that each of us is energy. Even when we die we still remain as energy. It is only the energetic body in which our soul was encased that is left behind. The essence of who we are becomes free of the body and is absorbed into the energy that we cannot see.

Based on the theory that our thoughts manifest things, if we do not let thoughts of the person or animal go, we are still manifesting them close to us. We may not be able to see them, but their essence is drawn back to us. This can work both ways. The person/animal who has died may be attached to you. They may wish to visit or be around you as they feel some kind of responsibility towards you. Some people are able to sense this themselves, while others go to Mediums and Psychics to get their answers.

This attachment of souls to each other can prevent either side from moving on fully. A part of their essence will linger in your consciousness and so even if they do move on, not all aspects of them will be present.

We have many aspects to our souls. Each part can become separated, creating a sense of incompleteness within. You may even feel this within you. By choosing to let others go and giving them permission to let you go, it allows them to be free to take the whole of their consciousness to wherever they choose to go.

If your relationship has been co-dependent with the person or animal that died, it can be particularly painful to let go of them. Up until the point of their death they provided all the love that you have been unable to give to yourself. When you decide to let this person go, it may be wise to consider ways to learn to love you so that you do not repeat this same need with someone or another animal again. Having a co-dependant relationship will always end up in heartache in the end because of the strong need and attachment to them to provide something to you and you to them.

Angels

Being aware of angels around me has helped bring comfort at the difficult times of accepting death.

Archangel Raphael is a great healer and can bring healing in your hour of need.

Archangel Azrael is the angel assigned to help people through death and the transition of death. He can help you with your grief and to reach a point of being able to release and let go of the pain and hurt that you feel.

To connect with either angel say their names and thank them for supporting you at this time. If you would like some words, you could say,

"*Thank you Archangel Azrael for your loving support during this time of losing (Name). I appreciate all the support and love that you bring. It provides great comfort to me to know that you are here with me.*"

When I sit in a funeral I say thank to Archangel Azrael for being with all who are there. The love and comfort that he can bring, helps to ease the suffering for all, particularly those who lack support and love from their family or peers.

During the night when I was comforting Lupa, I remember asking the angels for their loving support. I placed my hands on Lupa and asked that he be healed and that their love surround him. All I wanted was for him to be as comfortable as he could and to know that he was loved always. As I sang to him I trusted that the angels joined me in bringing the right words of comfort to him that eased his transition at this time.

When my brother was waiting to see if an operation was possible, during the night when it was my turn to watch over him I asked the angels to join me and to help bring him any healing or comfort that his higher self would allow. Having been told by the angels that he was to die I knew that this was an important time to draw them near so that they could support my brother on his journey and all those who were with me on theirs.

Angels are a great comfort. They bring a sense of peace with the love that they hold. If you allow yourself to be open to them, they can help you through your grief. You may not always be aware of them because your emotions are likely to cause an imbalance in your body's energy and so may prevent you from feeling them fully. However, knowing they are there is comfort enough if you can believe and trust this is so.

Crystals

During the time of my brother's passing, I brought with me a Rose Quartz to the hospital, offering this to my brother's wife, knowing the power and comfort it could bring. She may not have been aware of its energy because her emotions were raw, but the crystal would have provided comfort and healing on an energetic level.

Crystals have amazing qualities and healing and support is just one.

To help me to release any negative feelings each time I have experienced death, I have connected with my Amethyst, whose purpose is to help clear negative feeling energy.

Apache Tear is known as the "Grieving Stone" and can help support you through your grieving period.

Ruby can be used to help mend grieving that has impacted upon your heart. If you find that your heart feels broken and in need of loving support, a small piece of Ruby held in the hand or on a necklace or around you will help.

With these crystals, ask the crystal to connect with you, close your eyes and allow yours and the energy of the crystal to merge. You may not be sensitive enough yet to feel any vibrations from it. However, the intention to work with it and spending time connecting with it will enhance the possibility. Despite not feeling it the crystal will be working on an energetic level that your higher self will be aware of. To use them is therefore a matter of trust and to let go of any expectations you may have around them.

Summary

Everyone will experience death in accordance to his or her own understanding and beliefs of what happens when we die.

Trauma caused by death can result in shock that can sometimes have physical effects. This could include such things as, loss of speech, stuttering, inability to think about or do every day tasks, a shutdown of emotions and feelings of isolation. Using EFT you can begin to release these effects, allowing your body's energy to come back into balance.

Grieving is a natural process of letting go. Allowing yourself time to recover from the loss of a loved one is an important healing time. If you find comfort with the angels, they will help you through this, guiding you to words, people and healing activities that will assist you.

Anger is often an emotion that rises when grieving. Allow yourself to feel and let go of this as it comes. The Sedona Method (Details can be found on the Internet) is something I have come across recently that can be of help, as well as EFT.

Forgiveness is a great healer when letting go of old hurts with the person that has died. Carrying regrets and negative energy forward into your life will only cause you difficulty. See Things to do for a forgiveness exercise.

If you have no attachment to the person or animal that has died, only unconditional love, you may find the process of letting go much easier. However, it can take years of spiritual practice to reach this way of being.

Be patient with yourself and others who are grieving. It is better to let the emotions surface than to supress them inside. Surround yourself with white light while closing your eyes and meditating. This can help to bring comfort to you as you connect to all that is pure within.

Things you can do to help yourself

1. **Forgiveness**

To forgive anyone with whom you have felt hurt you can choose to write a letter to him or her that will not be seen by them. Write out all the things you want to say and why you feel the way you do. Be honest and write it exactly as it comes. Once written, put the letter away in a drawer until you are emotionally calm, as it is likely to have been an emotional journey while writing it. When you are ready, look at the letter to see the reality of what is written. Allow yourself to accept you in this moment or the person/animal and if you feel drawn to, do some EFT.

Taking the letter tear it up into little pieces and dispose of it in your bin. If you prefer you could choose to soak it in warm soapy water instead and mush it up so that it is no longer readable. As you do either say the words:

"I forgive you and I release you of all hurtful memories with love. I hold no un-forgiveness back. My forgiveness for you is total. I am free and you are free".

Again if you want to add, "*I love you*" this will add to the power of the forgiveness.

2. **Release and Let Go**

To release and let go of the essence of someone, find yourself a quiet room, sit comfortably and close your eyes. Bring all thoughts and memories of that person or animal into your mind.

You can have a photograph in your hand if that helps. Allow yourself to focus on them fully. When you feel ready say the following words:

"*I release all attachments to (Name). I choose to let all aspects of you go so that you may continue a complete life wherever you are. I love you dearly and will always remember the good times we had. I forgive anything you feel you need forgiving for and ask that you do the same for me. You are free to come and go whenever you choose. I am happy to let you go with my blessings and love.*"

3. **Emotional Freedom Technique**

Write out the names of all those you have lost, including animals. Going through the list, notice which ones still cause you to feel some upset when you think of them.

If you feel ready to release them, use the exercise above to let them go.

If you are still struggling to do so, write out some EFT statements to help. See **Appendix 2** for help with how to use EFT.

Examples of this might be:

Even though I am finding it hard to release and let go of (Name) I completely love and accept myself

Even though every time I think of (Name) I get upset I completely love and accept myself

Even though my heart feels broken at the loss of (Name) I completely love and accept myself

Even though I am finding it difficult to forget all the hurt felt by me from (Name) I completely love and accept myself

Even though I see no meaning to my life without (Name) here with me I completely love and accept myself.

There may be many other things you can think to say. Keep working on these until you notice a change in how you feel. The effects of EFT are not always noticeable straightaway, especially for deep hurts. The more you spend time working on them, the deeper it can work and the more at peace you will notice yourself feel.

4. **Memories - releasing**

If you are not sure what your thoughts are around a person/animal, spend sometime in mindful thought about them.

Sit somewhere comfortable. Close your eyes and focus upon your breath. As you breathe, think about the person/animal. Draw memories of them close to your mind. Notice what you are thinking as you stay focused on your breath. This will help to take the emotion out of the memory, allowing you to see the reality of what thoughts still remain. If they are negative, you can use EFT, or the forgiveness techniques above to help you release them.

Relationships - Love

My Story as I saw it then

When I was at school because of what others said about me I put other girls around me on pedestals and believed I was less worthy than them of having a boyfriend.

At 16 I had my first proper boyfriend - when I found out he was having his wicked way with another I ended it. After that I had one other before meeting my husband.

On the day I got married my mum commented that my fiancé and I were very different emotionally as people. I shrugged it off believing in love and all that it could bring. Of course, as mums often are, she was right.

Over time the difference between us became obvious. Two years after we were married I can remember standing on a dance floor thinking, what have I done. He was at home and I wanted to have fun. As I was only 22 it seemed a shame to not be sharing that with him. Believing in my marriage vows I decided to spend my time and energy doing a degree whilst working full time. My husband built a garage on the side of our home with his.

When my degree was nearing its end, I was ready to have children and so we agreed and did. Three children later it became more and more apparent that we were polls apart with our values and what we wanted from life.

After nearly 14 years of marriage a catalyst came into my life briefly, who made me aware of how unhappy I was. I asked my husband what he loved about me and for a second time, after asking a year before, he had no answer. This sent me on a downward spiral rushing into the hands of another very quickly after telling my husband it was over.

Emotionally I was a wreck and this new man gave me the attention and love I was craving. Quickly I agreed to move in with him to get out of the marital home, my children by my side.

This turned out to be a tricky and eventful relationship. He was suffering with depression and was very obsessive. Once he pinned me down angrily on the bed when I threatened to leave. I was vulnerable and in need. I stayed. We bought a house together and within a few months I said I wanted out. I drank red wine to null the pain of more turmoil and to keep the shouting from affecting me. The children sadly had no such barrier and at times had to listen and now can only remember this of him.

During the time I was making arrangements to move out one night I got drunk. My partner carried me upstairs, stripped me naked and took photos. I heard the camera and kept still, too drunk to do anything. I began to stir. Quickly he hid the camera under the bed so as not to get caught. His ex had warned me about him, which at the time I had ignored. This memory came into my head. I immediately thought of the girls when he went out of the room. Whilst he showered I checked their room. All was quiet. I snuck back and searched under the bed for the camera and hid it in a drawer. In the morning he was looking for it. I confronted him and made him delete the pictures. He said he was taking a memento!!

After this I got out as quickly as I could with my children.

Soon after a friend introduced me to a family member. We hit it off and again the relationship became intense quickly.

Not long after being together I saw that he had a low self esteem and suffered mild depression. He became very reliant on me finding it difficult to get work because of his shy character. Just before deciding to move South I ended things, only to be drawn back together a week before we left.

Five months after living down South with him I realised I was caring for another child. He still had no job and was doing little to change this so I ended things. He took it badly.

A month later he came to me begging for me to change my mind. He felt stripped of the chance to live down South. I said no. He threatened to come to my house. That night I stayed away from my house as the children were away. He broke into our back garden shed and found a tent and camped in our garden. He bleached I love You Sarah across the lawn.

It freaked me out when I returned. I didn't know what to do so I agreed to talk. For the next three months I agreed to let him to sleep on the settee whilst he sorted himself out a place to live down South. It took a further deadline to motivate him to take me seriously and finally he was out, in his own place with a job. He met someone quickly afterwards and I was relieved.

Pleased to be out of this relationship, but still needy of love, I met a businessman. He took me away on holidays and often treated me. It felt nice. However, he was pursuing another girl at the same time as dating me, asking me to hold in there whilst he made up his mind. I wasn't strong enough in myself at that point to end things hoping things would change. It did for a while.

One night when we both became drunk, he got violent with jealousy, his hands briefly round my throat over something there was nothing to be jealous of. I saw another side of him that left me distancing myself from him.

Not long after he had a breakdown. I stayed with him hoping things would improve. Eventually I grew tired of the difficulties and it came to an end. However, we have since remained good friends.

Still searching for love a friend introduced me to a man whom I immediately felt a bond with. He told me that day he was about to go bankrupt. I didn't care. The ideology of being with someone I felt a strong connection with overtook my mind.

Within about eight weeks we had agreed to move in together. This was to be another intense and passionate relationship. This time it was fraught with difficulty. He had depression, gambled and did nothing to help around the house. He pressed every emotional button possible within me. It was exhausting. Eventually one day I blew, sadly in front of his kids, the pressure being too much. He chose to walk.

Six months after moving house we were on the move again. The kids were not happy at this point and felt very unsettled. It caused many emotional outbursts to follow.

Madly, I still felt I loved this guy and was drawn back in for another round of 6 months of difficulty, this time living apart. One day my head was spinning so much I had no option but to end things.

You would think by now I would have learnt my lesson re rescuing lost souls and needing love. That was not to be. I fell for a guy who had literally just broken up from his marriage. His description of himself after his wife left was that he felt like a puppy that had had his nose slapped. I knew then he was weakened by his experience and unlikely to be strong enough for me.

But he was a dear sweet soul who had a broken heart and I thought I could fix it. We had two years together, me constantly being aware that he was not ready to commit properly to another relationship. He moved and bought a flat with his elderly mother, a place for him to retire. At this point I realised no matter how much love I had for him, he was not going to change. He was scared of living with someone again, or at least at this point. Also his wondering eye onto other women left me feeling very uncomfortable each time we went out. He was used to flirting with others as he and his wife had done this throughout their relationship - something that led to his wife being drawn to another, which was what ended their marriage.

There came a day when enough was enough and I plucked up the courage to end it, despite loving him.

A couple of weeks later another man leapt into my life giving me no time to recover. This became another intense and passionate relationship. At first it seemed perfect. One by one incidents occurred that revealed his true nature. He was very depressed and had become angry in his behaviour and outlook on life due to his difficult childhood experiences and failed relationships that had followed.

I loved him deeply and wanted so much to help him. To see him reach his best potential, since he was such a talented and clever man.

We had many major breakups where he said some very mean things to me. But the magnetism between us kept drawing me back in.

Eventually he moved abroad. I thought this would be the end but we still kept on finding each other in moments of need.

One day we committed our love to each other and decided to see how things could be but it was not long before all the doubts came in again. Being vulnerable and wanting reassurance, I told him I was having these doubts. He blew and ended things on Skype in front of my girls, again verbally nastily. They already didn't like him because of the persistent angry way they had witnessed him dealing with things over the relationship and so I accepted this time it was now over. Soon after he met someone else.

It was my most challenging relationship yet. I loved him dearly. The problem was, his temperament made him very tricky to be around and my reaction to it made it impossible to be vulnerable and feel safe with him. My home circumstances were also not suitable for this type of relationship. The timing was simply not in alignment for a long lasting relationship.

Once again I was on my own. This time however, I had become wiser and my awareness of myself had changed.

My Story as I see it now

Looking back over my story I can see that each relationship was a catalyst leading me to change. Each time I was in denial of the difficulties I had within myself. I reached out to others for love hoping they would be the answer to my happiness.

As time progressed and my awareness grew through my spiritual practice, it helped me to see the neediness and lack of self-esteem that I had for myself. Each time I embarked on a new relationship I carried on with it despite seeing early on the difficulties within it and the differences between us.

This behaviour highlighted a fear to commit, something my last boyfriend pointed out. Yet it was not in the way he intended. My fear to commit meant that I subconsciously chose relationships that I knew were likely to be temporary, despite my inner self wishing for something different.

Like Nanny McPhee in the film, I went into them knowing they needed and wanted me, and stepped out when the need was gone but the want was still there. I was fulfilling my need to feel some significance in my life, even though in reality I had this simply by being a mum.

This behaviour was not of course deliberate. This was how my computer had been programmed. I was drawn to men that were depressed and emotionally withdrawn and in need of some kind of help, a replica of my dad and my brother.

My need to provide a home for my children that was loving and settled became a saga of completely the opposite. When I look back, knowing what I know now, I can see that the Law of Attraction gave me what I had been seeking.

By focusing on the lack of support and love that I felt in my life from the male side of my family, the greater the lack became.

Each time that I put up with difficult and aggressive behaviour from others, I was denying my own self worth and my truth. There was no boundary set within me that recognised it as being wrong. It was a replica of behaviour that had happened towards me as a child. Had any aggression occurred towards the children, I would have walked immediately. They were merely onlookers. If I had love within myself it would have given me the strength not to accept the behaviour towards me and walk away if it continued.

Some of my behaviour could be seen as a need to control. Control not in an aggressive sense. More in a need to fit each person into a way of being that would suit the emotional needs of my children and me. Looking at it now, I can see that this was an impossible task and one that should never have been in my mind-set.

It is clear from my experiences that each person is unique and carries their own perceptions of the world based on their own stories. When two people come together, unless they are both able to completely let the past go, there will always be times when those perceptions clash.

Being as present as possible in a new relationship without memories and scars of the past allows each person to flourish and express themselves as their individual self. If your values and outlook are a good match it is likely there will be a strong chance of a harmonious relationship.

If you are able to communicate each time you are vulnerable, and feel safe doing so, you can walk past any difficulties and become stronger together. The more you can learn to appreciate one another, the greater the relationship will become.

By focusing on all that was wrong in a relationship I can see it simply created more of it to show my mind that it was right. To change this it is clear the opposite must occur. By Focusing on the positives and appreciating the good moments together, it enables the challenges to head into the past. It gives an opportunity each new day to build stronger foundations.

For example, when you get up in the morning, if your focus is on the negative argument you had with your partner that happened yesterday, it will affect how you feel about them in this day. This mind-set immediately creates a negative barrier between you and makes it hard to see them in a good light throughout the new day.

You can of course treat each day as a new day, but sometimes when things are unresolved it makes it difficult to do so. However, if you are able to see things from their perspective, you may find that you can turn things around sooner.

By letting go of the argument and reminding yourself of all the positive things your partner does when you wake up, you can change your feelings towards them creating a better day and a chance to resolve what happened.

Rushing into relationships based on chemistry I can see now is not a healthy way to proceed. Often this led into a trap, set by myself, as emotionally we became entwined liked ivy growing on the side of a tree. It became difficult to pull myself away, no matter what stormy weather came.

Through many painful breakups and challenging times, I have learnt that in the end the only person who can bring me happiness is me.

Once you have found happiness within you there is no longer an expectation that someone else will provide it. This frees your relationships to become more about the love and experiences you share rather than what you need from it. This also transfers into all relationships in your life.

Only when you are truly able to love who you are can you learn to love another unconditionally without judgment or expectation. By releasing the need for someone to fit into your ideal, you can enjoy them for who they are and what they bring. You can enjoy their individuality and learn to listen to their point of view without taking things personally. You can express your vulnerability freely and lovingly and they theirs with no fear of judgment. By feeling safe within yourself about yourself you can feel the same way with others. By trusting and loving yourself you can be the same with others.

Each person that is in our lives is reflecting to us emotions and views that we hold within. Sometimes it is hard to accept this and the victim in us uses it as a defence to get out of being in the relationship. I know because this is how I have been.

For example, when a person makes a comment aiming to help you in someway, if it awakens your hurt child from the past, your immediate reaction is to take it personally - to see it as criticism and to shun it away.

This is particularly true of children reacting to their parents when they have reached adulthood. It is also true within relationships.

I remember one incident with a boyfriend when we went to buy fish and chips from a local fish and chip shop. We had made our order and popped into the shop next door for some treats. When we went back the girl behind the counter had not wrapped the chips how he liked them. He reacted mildly aggressively, in a way like a child would who was not happy with something. She apologized and changed it. As we left I apologised to the girl. When we got home he was furious with me for undermining him. He felt I had not appreciated his point of view.

It was true I had not. As I saw it his behaviour was rude and out of order. I was merely speaking my truth and did not want the poor girl to be upset by his. I tried to explain this to him. He saw my behaviour as disrespectful, reminding him of his mother and the controlling nature of her he remembered. Needless to say, it led to one of the fallouts we had.

This constant difference in how we saw the world made it difficult to be together. We were both hurt children colliding together, wanting to be heard. Only when you realise this can you change it. It is too late for us - the damage is done.

Tools I have used to help me

Self Love

I cannot stress how important I have found this to be. Without it my relationships were simply not true to my partners or me.

Without self-love I could only love them with a need to be loved back to such a degree that this was an impossible task.

When you enter a relationship, of course there is not much point to it if one of you is not in love with the other. It creates an imbalance and eventually it falls apart. However, when you have a lack of love for yourself, no matter how much the other person shows you love your own feelings about you create doubt in what they say or do. It makes you question their intentions and look out for reasons why it should not work.

Loving another is about giving freely because you feel love for them. If that love is conditional it can easily be tainted by their reaction to the things you do. If it is unconditional your actions will be because you love them and not because of the reaction you wish to see. Without conditions they are free to be vulnerable and express themselves without fear of being judged. This freedom opens up opportunities for you both to experience something new and interesting that with conditions was not possible. It will inevitably deepen your experience of true love.

For example, when a boyfriend of mine paid for my hair to be done at an expensive hair salon I liked he thought he was being nice. My mind saw it as him not liking me as I was.

It was in fact me who was not satisfied with me and I often needed him to reassure me that I was lovable. Now I can see he simply wanted to make me smile and treat me to something I enjoyed. If I had loved me then I would have been able to fully appreciate the gesture and the results that came. Instead, I came home and cried, not liking the new look, and not liking me in that moment. I can only imagine the disappointment that he must have felt.

Emotional Freedom Technique (EFT)

Each day as I have become aware of my attachments to certain parts of my past around relationships, I have used EFT to help me to release them.

It has been particularly difficult to heal from my last relationship, despite knowing the challenges it held within. The reason for this has become apparent by using EFT to help.

He represented all of the past energies and challenges. His purpose was to bring them to my awareness so that I could heal myself from them. By letting him go it allows me to let go of the past and my previous thoughts on men. However, without these stories who am I? This is the fear I have had to overcome.

EFT has helped me to remove the hurt around the memories of the past and to accept that I can be without them. It has opened my mind to new possibilities seeing a possible future ahead that is very different from the past.

In the past I have struggled with being alone with no partner. Often I would cry because of it. This led me into the hands of those whose purpose it was to stir up what needed to be healed rather than attracting the long-term relationship I was hoping for.

By using EFT to work on my previous hurts, it has enabled me to begin loving myself. This has led to me being happier within allowing me to be content with being by myself. It has opened my mind to a different kind of relationship - one out of respect and love for myself as well as them. This new perspective enables love to flow more freely from an unconditional place rather than that of need.

Some examples of tapping statements I have used:

- *Even though I find it difficult having no partner I completely love and accept myself*
- *Even though I still feel attachments to my ex I completely love and accept myself*
- *Even though I am struggling to let the past go I completely love and accept myself*

There are many ways you can use EFT to help you in this area of your life. Being aware of how you are feeling and working through those emotions at the time of feeling them is one way you will learn to overcome them.

Angels

Since one of my biggest challenges is letting go of relationships despite knowing they are not right for me, I have often asked for help from the angels.

One of the difficulties with letting go is trusting that something better lays ahead. By working with the angels to clear attachments it has helped free my mind so that I can consider being be open to new things.

Archangel Michael is particularly great at helping in this area. He has a sword of light. You can ask him to help cut through any attachments with this, releasing you from any further thoughts or feelings around them. Michael's energy is strong and supportive. By believing in him and allowing him to help, it can help to speed up the process of letting go.

Archangel Raphael has also been amazing to work with in healing old hurts. Hurts can often be very deep. By asking Archangel Raphael to help release them and heal them, it can speed up the process of recovery from them. Sometimes to release them means to suffer some kind of illness first. Raphael can help to ease you through this and support you as you truly let it go.

Archangel Chamuel can help draw romance and love into your life.

Archangel Raguel can offer you guidance on creating harmony and better communication within your relationships. (See **Appendix 4** for more details as to how angels communicate with you).

Crystals

When times have been low and I have needed an extra boost of support, my crystals have played their part nicely.

Amethyst has helped to remove negative feeling thoughts and rebalance me when this has been my plight.

Carnelian especially when combined with orange calcite can help to elevate depression and SAD (Seasonal Affected Disorder). I have a sphere with these in and this has helped me particularly when I have felt disappointed and sad by a situation. I also feel Dragon energies combined in this crystal - this gives it a special purpose of helping to lift the user out of particularly dark thoughts and feelings.

Rose Quartz has helped me to connect to my heart and have the courage to let go of old hurts so that I can be open to love again.

Letting go of Judgment - Becoming Discerning

It is easy to hold judgment over yourself and others when relationships have failed or are failing. It is human nature to feel a need to place the responsibility somewhere.

However, judgment is destructive unless it is discerning. Discernment is judgment based on the truth and the reality of now. Judgment is based on the past and old perceptions.

By learning to be more present in the now, it has helped me to see the truth of how I am feeling and see the reality of what is happening. In the past I have had a tendency to latch onto only the good parts of what I saw in a person and see only this, denying the truth of the reality of what I was really experiencing with them.

This was based on a need for everything to be ok as I ignored the signs that it was me who needed to change.

Instead of seeing the truth and using it wisely, I held onto the judgments of the past, keeping myself safe in the situation, even though it was disruptive and unsettling.

To let go of judgment means to first become aware it is there. Once you are aware you can decide if it is based on reality or fiction.

For example, if you have been hurt in the past, perhaps someone has cheated on you, it is likely that your judgments of a new partner will be distorted from your past experience. You may send them a text or try calling them. If their response is not within the timescale you would expect, it could lead to you imaging them being with someone else in an intimate way. This is unlikely to be the truth. It is simply a story you are making up in your mind to justify their actions based on your truth of the past.

However, once the seed is sown unless you can come out of this cycle of thinking, it is unlikely that you will break free of it, and it will in the end destroy what you have with your partner.

Think of the Law of Attraction. What you focus on you create. If this is your focus it is likely that you will draw them into accepting that they may as well have an affair for nothing they say will change your perception of them - I have seen this happen with friends of mine.

By learning to keep your thoughts as positive as possible and focusing on all that is good in your relationship, you can learn to draw more of this in.

When you get a judgment that is based on your old story, be aware of it and let it go. You might like to write out your old story and tear it up afterwards into tiny pieces affirming that you are letting it go as you do. This often helps.

Letting go of Expectations

It is hard to be in a love relationship and not have some kind of expectation from the person you are living with. Each of us has a story in our minds of what we feel our life should look like. If the person you live with does not fit this in some way, your expectations of them lead to disappointment.

There are many ideals shown to us via film, media and others around us as to how a relationship could be. When we first set off to be with another, these form our basis and understanding of what to consider.

Expectations provide an immediate distortion of the mind. They create a story before the story has a chance to unfold. This story is a figment of your imagination. As the truth of the situation shows itself it may turn out not to reach your expectations and your illusion is shattered. The person before you has no chance since you are not able to see them for who they are, instead you can only see who you think they should be.

Letting go of expectations can therefore give you a blank sheet on which to begin creating your story. It will allow you to be present and to learn to love another for who they are in each moment. It will give you the opportunity to explore new ways of doing things that before had not reached your consciousness. It provides an opportunity for excitement and change.

Forgiveness

When things keep going in a different direction to what you wish for, it can be hard to forgive yourself when you finally see the reasons why. However, the past has gone. There is nothing that can be done to change it. The only time you have to focus on is now.

Forgiving myself for the calamity of errors that I seem to have created has been a tough part of my journey. It has been an important piece of the jigsaw in releasing and letting go of the hurtful feelings and allowing myself to love again.

When you carry around painful memories that you hold with another, it feels like a heavy burden and can weigh your energy down.

One way to practice forgiveness when relating to relationships is to imagine the person sitting in front of you on a stage. The spotlight is upon you both. Feel yourself connecting with the person's heart by opening your heart energy and focusing on theirs.

As you connect think back to the painful memories that you share. Ask for forgiveness from them for any hurt you may have caused them. When it feels right, say to them that you forgive them for any hurt they have caused you. Also send forgiveness to yourself for anything you feel negative about towards yourself from this relationship.

Allow yourself to feel a sense of peace as you let go of the negative energy that has been surrounding this issue and relationship.

If there is more than one relationship in which forgiveness is needed, spend time doing this for each.

Letting go and Releasing

One of the reasons I found it so difficult to end relationships was due to my own fear of the unknown if I were to release and let them go.

By releasing and letting them go it meant I had to face myself - be by myself until someone else came along.

This fear simply led me into more of the same - relationships that were full of challenges and hurt.

Now that I have had time to reflect on my relationships and can see what I have been doing, I can appreciate the benefits of letting them go.

By holding onto them, it would have meant keeping myself back - not allowing myself to change and move to more positive times.

Releasing old energies and memories is rewarding and gives you the chance to reinvent who you want to be. It allows you time to heal your old wounds and to create the space for love.

Learning to love you and accept who you are lessens your need to become attached to other individuals. Instead it gives you a greater scope to enjoy the process of choosing rather than feeling the need to stay in something that does not feel good.

To let a relationship go means to see the reality of a situation and accept it entirely instead of creating ifs and maybes, which is very easy to do.

If there is someone you need to let go from your past, imagine them standing in front of you. Look into their eyes and say to them how much you love them. Let them know that despite your love for them you can see they are ready for new experiences and explain that you are to. Be happy for them. Hug them and watch as they walk away from you. The further they walk away, feel yourself detaching more from them. See them as a small dot in the distance and when you are ready let the dot go.

You may have to do this a few times if your connection to them is deep. You could also ask Archangel Michael to help you break any cords or attachments from past lives that could be keeping you linked together. (See **Appendix 4** - Angels for an explanation about Michael).

Another option is to have a small goodbye ceremony in your own space. Have a picture of them, surround it with things they love and you love. Say special words to them as you would at a funeral. Buy flowers, drink a toast and bury the picture or soak it in warm soapy water, mushing it down and releasing them as you do.

Summary

Relationships are part of your journey to get to know yourself better. Sometimes they can last for a lifetime. Other times they are temporary, leading you to better times once you understand yourself more clearly.

The more present you are in a relationship, the easier it is to be real and vulnerable within it. If your thoughts are often drawn to the past, it can create circumstances within your mind that are imaginary only. If focused upon, these stories can eventually lead to your relationship ending, especially if your new partner is mistrusted as a result.

Having expectations of your partner can put extra pressure upon the relationship. If your expectations are not met it can cause disappointment leading to arguments or difficulties that will challenge the love you have.

True love is unconditional. It allows you both to be vulnerable and wholeheartedly yourselves. It gives you both the opportunity to explore your own self without the fear that the other will take it personally.

A relationship is about giving. If you enter it with the intention to see what you can get from another, it is likely to cause you disappointment. No one is responsible for supplying you with happiness. It is not possible. Each of you is individual and as such has your own unique thoughts, feelings and perceptions.

Things you can do to help yourself

To help relationships become more loving in your life first it is important to acknowledge that you are the creator.

1. **Reflection**

Taking a blank sheet of paper, think about all your past relationships. These can be with family and love relationships. Write out the names of those you have had challenges with. Spend time writing out the pros and cons of each of these relationships. When you have finished compare the results. What seems to be the common thread throughout? Looking at yourself, taking responsibility for this, what is it reflecting to you that you need to change within you?

For example, if others are showing you disrespect, how are you disrespecting yourself? If others are not valuing and appreciating you, how can you begin to value and appreciate yourself?

2. **Vision Board**

Thinking of your love relationships, write down all the good things you have experienced. What parts of the relationships have you enjoyed?

Making a vision board, create an image of the type of partner you wish to attract into your life at this time. What do they look like? How old approximately would you like them to be? Are they to be a family person? What are your values? Do you wish theirs to match these? Write down all the things you have enjoyed within other relationships around them and add to these the things you would also like to invite into a new relationship.

Now looking at yourself, if you were this person, would you be attracted to you? Considering where you are at, whom do you need to become in order to attract this person into your life?

3. **Emotional Freedom Technique**

Using EFT begin to work on some of the blocks you have found in the two exercises above. Write out some statements that cover the issues and begin to tap. As you tap you will often find that other things come into your awareness that will help you to deepen the healing. The deeper you are prepared to go the greater the healing and the more change you will find in your new relationships going forward.

4. **Forgiveness**

Going back to the section on Forgiveness, use the exercise given to help forgive yourself and others for hurts you have suffered as part of your past.

The more people you can do this with in mind, the greater the healing. Forgiveness is often the very thing that holds many back from being able to have a harmonious relationship in the future. Without it, you will keep reliving the past and stay in the same kind of relationships you have had previously.

5. **Releasing and Letting Go**

If you have been struggling to let go of a person and memories of them keep making you sad, carry out the exercise given in the Releasing and letting go section.

If you carry people forward into your future, it will distort all new relationships until you let them go. Letting negative experiences go will free space in your mind to be open to new positive ones.

Parenting

My Story as I saw it then

Becoming a parent was a dream come true - I was so excited each time that I gave birth to a new baby, all three being born within four years. Determined to give them a good start, I breastfed each of them, despite with the first having a few challenges to overcome. My determination ensured that I succeeded. It was a gift I was able to give that has stood them in good stead health wise.

The problems in parenting began when my husband shared different values to me. His ideal would have been for me to return to full time work. Mine was to stay at home and be a good supportive loving mum.

It was important to me to obtain jobs that allowed me to take the children with me. When I did choose to do something at the weekend, my husband often complained about having to give up his time to look after them. One time I went to a job interview to get better pay feeling ill from a bug only to be told by my husband when I got it that he did not want me to work the weekends any more. He didn't want his free time used up to look after his children.

After a while of not feeling supported by my husband and unloved we became slowly distant from one another.

When we first separated I started full time work and he shared some of the responsibility of childcare as the children and I now lived a long way from their school. I would drop the children to him on my way to work at 7.30am. It was a challenging time but was only for a short while.

When I moved South with the children, at first my ex husband would have them once a month. Driving them to a halfway point my ex would take them to the Midlands from there. This worked well for a while, keeping some kind of contact with their dad.

Then he announced he was going to live in America. This was hard on the children. Now their contact was limited to the odd Skype call and a visit once a year. After a while the Skype calls lessened and only the odd text or message was exchanged.

As I challenged myself with one relationship after another, hoping to find the right man to be part of our lives, things became stressful at times. My unhappiness causing me to be less patient and easily upset by comments made by my children as I took them personally.

After one particular period of upheaval, moving twice within 6 months, the children became unsettled. We went through a period of disagreements and testing of my resilience. I remember shouting a lot as I tried to defend myself in amongst what was being said. It was hard dealing with the challenging behaviour of teenagers on my own. Although I had a boyfriend during some of it, they were not able to intervene, as they did not live with us.

I remember one time getting so upset I drove to Poole Quay in the middle of the night just to get away from what was going on.

In 2011 I had a spiritual awakening which brought my awareness to a new way of seeing things. So began an exploration of new things that brought me tools and an understanding that helped me to see through this behaviour and begin to change things around.

Remembering back to one incident, one of my daughters was in a rage because I refused to let her have a shower, which was situated in the en-suite in my bedroom, at 11.30pm. Explaining my reasons emotionally and defensively I went into my bedroom and sat with my Rose Quartz crystal. After a while she came into my room and raged again. The crystal had helped to calm me back to my rational self - **The Safety Zone**. In this new calm state I didn't respond as I had earlier causing her reaction to change. She calmed down and began to cry, explaining the things that were on her mind. I kept quiet offering her my loving support. The next day I arranged some counselling for her at school as agreed by her.

The more I was able to see the children's behaviour as their own and less of a personal attack on me, the easier it became to deal with what came.

Whilst we were going through the more difficult times, I remember feeling alone and unsupported.

Neither my family nor my ex was around to offer any comfort. The wellbeing and welfare of my 3 children was totally my responsibility. This felt huge at the time, especially as I stepped into self-employment so that I could free my time to be there when required.

My Story as I see it now

My desire to have children was to fulfil a need within me to be a mum. Having them is the best thing I have done in my life so far.

They have taught me so much about myself and about life. Watching each of them develop and grow, despite the challenges we have encountered together, has been rewarding and enlightening.

Looking back I can see my husband was leading me to look at myself. To take steps to learn to love me. If he had provided me with a loving experience I would never have seen or experienced what was wrong within me.

The lack of support and feeling of loneliness that I had was creating more of the same. The more I felt it and focused on it the greater it showed itself. These were aspects of me being reflected back to me - I did not need others to fulfil what I could do for myself.

By learning to love me it has taught me to value my own company and to enjoy simply being me. It has helped me to appreciate my life and those within it.

As I have learnt to appreciate myself and my life more it has opened up the opportunity to let go of expectations. By letting go of expectations it has enabled things to flow more freely into my life that before were being blocked by my own thoughts of hardship and difficulty.

My negative view of what was happening with my children was encouraging more negativity to occur. As the Law of Attraction shows us, what we focus on we create.

When I changed my perspective and stopped acting like a hurt child, it allowed me to take on the role of parent not only to my children but also to myself.

As a hurt child and victim of my own thoughts, I acted the victim in my life attracting drama and circumstances that simply created more of it.

As I learnt to love me it enabled me to become discerning rather than judgmental. The truth of what was happening became apparent removing the programme of the past that I had created.

It helped me to appreciate my children more for whom they were individually rather than how I expected them to behave. This altered my perception, allowing me to give them the freedom to develop their own views and experiences of the world without me dictating to them what should be according to how I saw things. Although at times this has been hard, since I have not always agreed with their choices, I understand now that we each have our own ability to choose and it is important to respect others in making theirs.

As a parent what most of us want for our children is the best for them. However, their own unique view of the world means that what they see as best for them is not necessarily a match to your opinions.

As part of my growth I can see that children simply want to be loved for who they are. They do not wish for their own inadequacies to be revealed to them. In fact by focusing on loving them and encouraging them, they face their own inadequacies sooner as they see them for themselves.

For example you can tell a child that playing on their computer for long lengths of time is not good for them. That the energy they are spending time in and the focus of the games they are playing is affecting their view of the world and themselves. However, until they are ready to see it for themselves, your words can simply be likened to a parrot nagging in their ear.

Again referring back to the Law of Attraction, what you focus on you create - the more I focused on their negative behaviour, the more it became a reality.

Letting go of the focus and encouraging them to do other things instead is a better way to draw them away and give them the opportunity to explore something different.

My children taught me this lesson when they kept warning me that a particular partner was not good for me and then gave up after several times of seeing us coming back together. By them giving up it changed the energy of it and made me have to face the truth by myself. Once I saw the truth I could finally walk away.

My children have therefore taught me compassion. We have each learnt how to be compassionate and love one another despite the individual journeys we are all choosing for ourselves.

Tools I have used to help me

Law of Attraction

One of the biggest lessons from being a parent is seeing the Law of Attraction in action. Looking back I can see how many times, if I had known of this, I could have turned things around simply by seeing things differently.

The Law of Attraction states that your vibration and thought is a match to whatever you wish to create.

For example, if you wish to create children who tidy up the home without having to nag at them, you need to first believe it is possible. Whilst your thoughts and vibration focus on their laziness and untidy ways, it simply draws more of this into your experience.

By learning to appreciate each little thing they do to help, it builds their self-esteem. Gradually they associate helping with good feelings rather than being nagged at. This gradual change will enable them to begin to enjoy tidying up rather than seeing it as a chore as their values will come to match yours.

You could sit for a while and simply visualize a tidy home, with the children tidying up as they go. As this becomes your thoughts and belief the experience that you receive will become a match to this.

When I focused on feeling unsupported in my life, I failed to notice and truly appreciate any little moments of support that appeared. By not appreciating them, it kept my vibration low in this area of my life and so the only match for this was to provide more of it.

Think of the Law of Attraction like planting seeds. If you plant a seed in stony ground, where there is little nutrition and neglect it because of how negative you feel it is likely to wizen and die.

If you plant the seed in fertile soil, full of nutrition and spend time loving and nurturing it, the plant is likely to flourish and grow strong and vibrant.

If therefore your thoughts are negative and full of sadness, the seeds that they sow will become a match for these. The experiences you receive as a result will be negative and sad leaving you feeling worse than before. Any dreams that you have of succeeding will begin to feel out of reach.

If your thoughts are loving, nurturing and positive, the seeds that match these will flourish. The experiences you receive as a result will inspire and encourage you to sow more. This can only be achieved if first you believe and love yourself for by doing so this becomes your automatic state of consciousness.

When something is automatic, it requires no effort. Instead all thoughts become a match to it.

If therefore your life is presently one of difficult challenges and expectations, ask yourself, what is your automatic state of flow?

When you enter details into a search engine on the Internet what you get back will be dependant on what you wrote. For example, if you write divorced, lonely parent you will get things back that match this request. If you write single parent looking for inspiration the response will be quite different.

Your thoughts are the same as this and the universe responds to them just as quickly. So being aware of your thoughts using **The Safety Zone** can be very helpful in changing your view of parenting.

When considering your thoughts as you parent your children, the same applies. For example, when you throw negative comments and experiences at a child, the outcome often is a child who lacks self esteem and feels of no value in the world.

When surrounding them with love, encouragement and inspiration, it will give them every opportunity to grow as they wish to develop, having the confidence in themselves to do so.

Self Love

However you experience yourself in the world, others will always reflect this back. Since children are the closest relationship you will often have, they provide the greatest gift of this.

When you experience behaviour from your children that you do not like it is often teaching you something about who you are. How you respond to it shows you how vulnerable and sensitive you have become to it.

As a parent if you are not able to love yourself, your behaviour reflects this out to others. Your children pick up the signs and this becomes their role model for themselves. No matter how much love you may throw at them, your example of how to be towards yourself sets an image in their mind that they believe to be true.

Learning to love me has been a journey of discovery. Before I was not able to see how lacking love for me was impacting on my life. I was too involved in my story and had accepted that this was who I was. It did not occur to me that I might be able to change it and consequently change my life.

As I have begun to love me the more positive the change that has showed itself in all areas of my life. Happily I can say that as a parent my aim is to become a new and inspirational role model to my children. By changing my life whilst they are still young and at home it has given them an alternative perspective to witness.

At first I accept they may not see the benefits, but after a while of watching the results they have the opportunity to explore what has made the difference, especially since they have memories of the past to compare to now.

It is important not to have regrets for the past, for you cannot change what has happened. Each of you in the family will have experienced things from your own perspective and will have the opportunity to learn from it. Without such experiences life would become stagnant and what you learn from it may not be enough to help you become the best you can be.

The only thing I can change is how I parent my children now. What inspiration and love I can give to them that will encourage them to be the best of themselves. I am thankful that I am able to see life from this perspective, for this has taught me to appreciate every step of their journey. To take notice of the little things and watch as each step builds into something amazing for them. This is an everlasting journey as part of my life with them and it is a true gift to have such an opportunity to experience a positive evolving changing life with them and all it brings.

Emotional Freedom Technique (EFT)

EFT as we have discussed before is useful for healing old hurts and pain both externally and within.

During my time as a parent so far there have been many challenges we have faced due to the journey we have been on. Each time that I become aware of a negative emotion within me as a result of this, I now have a tool that is easy to use that can be utilised to rid myself of the negative vibration the memory carries.

EFT helps me to connect more to each day. This helps me to see what the reality is of my behaviour and thoughts. As I notice the reality it gives me the opportunity to change it if it does not suit what I want.

The more sad and hurt I feel when affected by an experience, the deeper I can see the pain is. EFT is great for reaching into the depths of a problem and resolving what needs to be seen. As your mind becomes clearer and your heart more open as a result of the healing it brings, it allows you to move forward more positively to what you want to create.

Using EFT has helped me to become a better parent. It has increased my awareness of my own negative thoughts and feelings. As I have dealt with challenges within me it has improved my relationship with my children.

Angels

Angels are beings of light full of nothing but love. By working with them through problems and when manifesting new things, there is always the reassurance of knowing that they are not judging you.

Whatever you wish for they will help you to create, simply because they know that the experience and circumstances that are formed, will bring the next lesson you want to learn.

Sometimes we cannot always see this and think they are not with us when a storm suddenly shows itself. However, this storm is often the clearing that is needed in order to see clearly what it is you are bringing into your awareness.

For example, you may wish for a partner that you know is not right for you to change in some way so that you can be with them. The angels will help instigate an experience that will help to remind you of the reasons it will not work or highlight an opportunity to change your perspective, encouraging you to see the positives of your partner.

You may wish for your child to stop smoking or drinking. Asking the angels for help with this may take your child into a situation that will challenge your beliefs as you see them struggling. You may wish for a miracle but sometimes that miracle can only happen if the person is shown another perspective first.

For example, the child or a close friend of theirs or even a celebrity they follow may first have to suffer some kind of illness in order to bring their awareness as to how dangerous what they are doing is to their health. Until this warning comes, your words are simply that, just words. They lack meaning for the impact of them is not as great as an experience of the reality of what they are doing.

When a child is knocked down on their bicycle with no helmet and sustains injury, all those who know the child suddenly become aware of how important it is to wear a helmet. Real life examples are therefore very powerful in instigating change within others.

When your child is poorly focusing on Archangel Raphael can help to bring extra comfort and healing to them. Encouraging your child to focus on the colour green can help to enhance the connection.

Archangel Metatron can help where your child has physical challenges. This might be if your child is particularly sensitive. Metatron can help guide you to resources and people that can help.

Archangel Gabriel is particularly interested in helping parents along with Mother Mary. If you find you have worries and concerns around your parenting or your children, ask Gabriel and Mary to step in and guide you. Remember to say Thank you at the beginning as if the help is already there.

Archangel Gabriel can also help with conception if you are having difficulty in conceiving or want support in letting go of the thoughts and fears around previously difficult births.

These light being's purpose is to help bring greater clarity to your experiences so that you can connect to a deeper knowledge within. By trusting in them you can enhance yours and your children's lives and create deeper more loving experiences.

Crystals

As mentioned in my story I found my crystals to be of great use to me when changing my reactions to situations. The energy that they have been able to give to me during times of crisis has helped to replace my own negative energies of the past with support and love.

This support and love, which before I felt was lacking, has helped bring me to a new perspective and view of myself. It has enabled me to see things more clearly and to be happy to let the past go.

Working with crystals when you are particularly upset, for example, while in **The Safety Zone**, can help you to elevate the negative feelings faster. This can speed up your ability to respond to a situation from a rational perspective rather than an emotional one. This is particularly important when dealing with your children, as it will help you to act from an adults point of view rather than that of your hurt child, based on your past experiences.

Carrying a small piece of crystal of your choice in your pocket will immediately give you something to reach for in a crisis that will help to calm your mind and bring you back to focus. The more you practice this outside of a crisis the more natural it will feel when one comes.

There are many different crystals that can help support you and your children through minor and big challenges. If there is currently a challenge you would like help with spend some time researching which crystal will offer the most help. Small pieces of crystal are often reasonable to buy and the value they offer is priceless. (See **Appendix 5** for some basic uses of crystals)

Letting go of Judgment

It is easy to judge oneself as a parent, especially when you can see the impact of your own behaviour on your children and how different you wish it could have been. However, to judge means only to cause negativity and this will do nothing but destroy the potential of now.

Each moment that you have in your life is an opportunity to create things as you want. If you keep on judging yourself or others based on the past and what you think others want, you are not focused on the reality of now.

Judgment comes from a story created in your mind. For example, you may phone one of your children when you are out believing them to be at home. When they don't answer, your mind begins to create a story. This story can be based on many things, but often it will draw your thoughts into it a belief that is negative.

The longer the silence goes on the greater the worry becomes and the story becomes real. As the story you have created becomes real it brings with it anxiety and negative energy.

When you get home you see your child is fast asleep with their headphones on. They had no way of hearing your call.

All your worry and anxiety is based on a judgment that you made of them based on the silence that was created. This can sometimes cause a negative response when you see the reality of what happened. Your exhaustion from the worry may cause you to become agitated and no longer in the rational mind.

Judgments made of your children are often based on your own perspective of how you wish them to be. Each child is unique. Their perception of the world and how they experience your behaviour towards them will be based on how sensitive and aware they are. The greater their sensitivity and awareness, the more easily they will be upset by any negative judgments made of them.

Learning to accept your children for who they wish to be helps them to become confident and loving towards themselves. When you find yourself judging your children, sometimes this can turn into controlling behaviour from you, which often causes stress and strain on your relationship with them.

The more you can practice letting go of the judgment and allowing your children more freedom in their choices, the greater chance they will find fulfilment within themselves at an earlier age.

Letting go of Expectations

Expectations of your children and of yourself, causes nothing but difficulty and harm. Each time an expectation is made, it creates a limitation on the outcome. It gives no leeway for freedom of choice or individuality. The energy it portrays is negative when the expectation is not met.

For example, if you have high expectations of what you wish your children to achieve when at school they will immediately pick up on your disappointment when this does not happen. Even if you think you have handled things well, your energy and the words you express will give a negative undertone that will have a knock on effect on your child. It is likely they will already have set their own expectations based on how you handled things before. This consequently may cause them to be disappointed in themselves if they think they have not reached your expectations. Your words of disappointment will only enhance this and continue to effect the way they look at themselves.

If instead you let go of your expectations and praise the child no matter what the outcome is, it is more likely they will listen to your guidance when encouraging them to look at ways to get better results if that is what they want. Making it about their wishes gives them the power to do it for themselves.

Allowing each day to be special for what it can bring, will give you a greater appreciation of life. As you appreciate your life more you will also appreciate those within it sharing a deeper respect and love for one another.

No day is ever the same. The energy of the universe changes within every second. Over a 24-hour period the energy shifts greatly. The energy of a planet is particularly powerful for it is more intense. If one part of the world is having a particularly challenging time, this energy enters the consciousness and spirals across into all.

Imagine the earth as you. Each experience that the earth is having is affecting some aspect or part of you, albeit not on a conscious level.

Effectively this is what is happening to everyone all of the time. Therefore not only are we responsible for our own wellbeing in the way we live our lives, but we are also responsible to the consciousness as a whole.

Each thought that you have is impacting not only on your own circumstances but also on those around.

If for example you are focusing on a child in Africa that is starving or a homeless person who is hungry, your likely reaction is to provide a temporary solution to their problem and to feel sad for them. However, if this is all anyone did, these people would remain as they are and continue to have a sad energy supporting them.

By changing your focus to look at the bigger picture, you will begin to see solutions as to how the situations of these people might be changed for the better. By changing your expectations of them and seeing them in a different light you can begin to bring out the best in them. The more people who do this the greater the chance of positive change.

By seeing the child as poor and starving, your mind is automatically sending thoughts that keep on creating this unless it looks at the potential of the situation to change instead. Negative thoughts are limiting whereas positive open thoughts allow positive opportunity for change.

This is the same for yourself and that of your children. Seeing you or your child as failing and struggling creates an image that holds this expectation. If instead you could see yourself or your child as doing the best that you or they could do in this moment based on yours or their mind-set and experiences around you or them, it opens the opportunity for positive change.

Without expectations your mind is free to express itself as things happen without any negative undertones.

By encouraging your children in all aspects of themself, it gives them the confidence to excel in the things they love to do rather than having to follow in the footsteps of what others expect of them.

Forgiveness

Without forgiveness it is impossible to move on past times that have been painful.

Forgiving others for causing physical harm to you can be very difficult if they took advantage of your vulnerability at the time. However, all experiences are given as learning opportunities. The very act of forgiveness is a lesson in itself.

When forgiveness is not given it is like carrying the puss in a spot around with you under the surface of your skin, always waiting to erupt in some way.

No matter who it is that brings your awareness to it, the reaction to them will be based on the old experience received rather than the reality of what is happening. Sometimes the event that is happening is a repeat of the original experience. This can be because this is what you have come to expect.

Sometimes your children can be caught in the middle of this reaction through no fault of their own. Their behaviour in that moment is simply a reminder of what happened and this causes you to erupt. It may also be that your reaction is the opposite and causes you to become controlling in an attempt to prevent them having the same experience.

Letting old painful memories go lightens your energy and heals any sores. It allows you to create new experiences that no longer remind you of the old. It gives you the opportunity to bring up your children without the scaring of the past distorting your reactions towards them.

Often forgiving yourself is the hardest task, given that your judgment of you is likely to be harshest of all. This is especially so if your behaviour has impacted upon the way you have or are bringing up your children.

Taking your mind to a place that can see the innocence of who you are beneath all your experiences will help.

Using meditation/mindfulness, imagine yourself as a young child. If it helps, look at an old photo of you. Looking at you as an innocent child, say loving words of encouragement to yourself. Say that you forgive you for all thoughts and feelings that may have led to difficult challenges you have faced or are facing now. Ask yourself to always see the positive of all experiences so that you may pass through them easily and freely. Surround yourself with a coat of magic, something that you can remember. Say a word or sentence also to yourself that is encouraging, loving and supportive.

When you come back to reality, use this image of the coat and the words or sentence to keep yourself in the present moment, reminding yourself to see the positive of all that is happening in today.

Summary

Being a parent carries with it huge responsibility. Those in your care will often follow patterns and beliefs that you introduce them to.

If as a child you did not receive encouragement and love as you would have liked it maybe that you are not able to express the same to your own children, as they would like. This is not because you are a bad parent but simply the consequences of never being taught how.

Parenting yourself and loving you can help you to become a better parent with your children.

Small gestures of appreciation of your child's work and the things they do can go a long way to helping them feel loved.

According to the Law of Attraction, the vibration that you send thoughts out into the universe will affect the creation you intend. If therefore you wish to change something that is negative, such as difficult behaviour, it is best to stay focused on a positive outcome. By not responding to the behaviour negatively, for example by taking it personally and being defensive, the person will have to eventually face themselves.

Providing a loving response will encourage them to feel valued and help them to see some good in themselves despite the challenges they feel they are facing.

Facing them together and coming up with a positive solution will help them to feel you are on their side.

Holding onto expectations based on your upbringing or how you think children should behave, can have a negative effect on your own children's behaviour. Allowing each child to be individual and unique will help them to explore their own self and appreciate who they are much more quickly than if you try to force them to be someone they are not.

Judgments based on your own perception of how you see a child can tarnish your relationship with them. Children are not here to be replicas of you. They have come to experience the world and express themselves within it at their own individual unique self. If you judge them for the way they are, this is a reflection of yourself in some way. The more you focus on any negative judgement the greater the harm to your relationship is likely to be.

Teaching a child to thrive in the now and encouraging them in all they wish to do will enhance their self esteem and give them the confidence to face the world when they become adults.

Sometimes what children achieve will take you out of your comfort zone as you begin to see the potential that lies within you. Rather than putting the handbrake on in fear of what will be, embrace this and begin to make positive changes within yourself. As you do this will encourage your children to reach even higher.

Things you can do to help yourself

Each of you will have experienced different things as part of being a parent. The ideas below are to give you something to help clear any old hurts that may be obscuring your view of your relationship with your children in this present moment. The aim is to enhance your relationship with them.

1. **Reflection and Forgiveness**

Find a photo of each of your children when they were very young, possibly even just born. Spend time with each one exploring their faces and seeing the innocence of them.

For some you may find this difficult, if the birth was challenging or you feel some kind of resentment towards them for changing your life. If either of these applies use the example given under the forgiveness section to work on forgiveness with them. Recognise that all thoughts you have are based on your own choice of perspective. You can change this perspective any time to create a better and more positive outcome. What you believed back then may be different to how you see things now. Or perhaps, looking at the innocence and vulnerability of them will help you to see they were simply that, blank sheets of pureness waiting for experiences to be shared to help bring the best out of them.

If your troubles are more recent with your children and they are older, seeing their innocence and reminding yourself that we are each an example of the experiences we have received in the world, will help you to look past what is happening now.

If your child is replicating your behaviour or is highlighting the lack of love you have for yourself, thank the child in the picture for their part in liberating you now.

2. **Law of Attraction**

Write out on a piece of paper exactly as you see your children now. Be totally honest. Do not spend time contemplating the question. Simply write what first comes into your mind.

Take a break to allow your emotions to settle and come back to the paper. Read aloud to yourself what you have written.

Thinking about the Law of Attraction, what could you change about the outlook you have of them that will begin to create a different outcome from them?

For example, if you have described them as lazy, could you see that their time is simply spent on things they love to do rather than on what your expectations are of them? By changing your perspective you are no longer treating them as a lazy person. Instead you begin to treat them as capable of doing things. Praise them each time that they do something small that is productive. As you build up the praise eventually they will see themselves as capable and no longer fit themselves into the category you previously gave them - that of being lazy.

3. **Old Patterns**

If you are currently struggling in your life, spend some time reflecting on your thoughts. For one week begin journaling your feelings.

Note down what you have felt throughout the day; Examples are disappointed, unsupported, unloved, elated, joyful or any other expression of emotion. You can do this at the end of a day with a cuppa so that you feel relaxed while doing it.

When you get to the end of the week take a look at what you have written. Look at the patterns of thought. See how many days match one another.

Looking at yourself in the mirror, ask yourself if you feel these things about yourself personally? Is it that you feel disappointed with who you have become? Do you feel as if you cannot support yourself and so need encouragement from others? Do you love yourself? Are you happy with your life and have a sense of fulfilment?

Once you have answered these questions, take a look at how your behaviour towards yourself is reflecting to your children.

Decide how you might change this outlook, one day at a time, so that you can change the outcome to something more positive.

4. **Sensitive Children**

Children that are sensitive are often easily upset or show symptoms through allergies. These children often need nurturing in a different way that allows them to be confident in their sensitivity. Encourage them to do activities that involve being creative so that they can explore ways to express themselves.

Meditation or mindfulness and crystals are often tools that they will relate to and be keen to use to help support their sensitive outlook.

5. **Emotional Freedom Technique**

Becoming aware of yourself more can help you to see how you are behaving as a parent. Spend time observing your expectations and judgments of yourself and others. Write them down. Thinking back to your own upbringing, write out statements that you feel have been said to you or expressed to you in some way that may have led to this behaviour.

Using EFT take these statements and tap through the sequence until you feel the negative feelings become dormant. (See **Appendix 2** for further help on using EFT)

A week later, observe you again and see what judgments or expectations repeat themselves, if any, or what new ones arise. Again writing out statements use EFT to help clear them. Repeat this weekly until you feel happy with the response.

Eventually you will notice your thoughts and feelings will have changed and consequently this will naturally improve the way you parent your children.

In time you will see this new reflection having a positive impact on your children and the way they feel about themselves.

Money and Finances

My Story as I saw it then

When I was young I remember the subject of money was never an easy one at home. Money was often tight and restricted.

As soon as I was able I got myself a paper round to give myself some spending monies.

As I got married money remained tight. I was new into my job and the wages were very low. Over time my wages increased, the company I worked for agreed to pay for my studies and things were beginning to feel a little freer. Then I chose to have a family. Giving up work meant a cut in our income by almost half and despite doing many part time jobs that allowed me to spend time with the children, income was still limited. We did not go without but lived like many do at this stage of our lives on a tight budget.

When we divorced through my own guilt of being the one to make the choice, I settled for what my ex would give rather than going to a solicitor as I did not have the funds to do this.

Over the next ten years I managed money as best I could. I used credit cards to help provide what was needed. My savings disappeared as I paid the rent (which doubled when we moved down South) and other living expenses. When I became self-employed as a mortgage adviser my income quickly dropped as the mortgage crash came.

After a while I found I had used every resource I had up, I was heavily in debt and needed to pay the rent, so finally I signed onto Housing Benefit. We nearly lost the house we were in at the time, but I managed to convince the landlords to let us stay. Even with debts piling up I was determined to stay self-employed, believing in my dream. I also wanted to be at home to support my children's welfare, since there were no family members around to help.

Admitting I needed help with Housing Benefit was difficult at the time. I remember standing in the benefit room feeling ashamed of myself for letting things come this far.

In 2011 I opened a new business called Aspire2bfree. I worked hard doing many different types of work to bring income in. Most years following produced a low income but I believed in what I was doing and felt at some point income would rise. Without the benefits and maintenance from my ex (which he kept low) and help from my mum as a guarantor we would have been forced to look into council housing of some kind.

Accepting this low income we lived accordingly. Keeping the end goal always in my mind of succeeding in my business and meeting someone who would share a life with my children and me was the dream that kept me going.

For many years since we have lived month to month. I looked at being employed, and did do some part time work, but my determination to see my business grow made it ok to live this way.

As the children have grown up the income has reduced from benefits and maintenance, but somehow with the help of others, especially my mum who has often stepped in during emergencies for which I am very grateful, I have managed to keep us afloat in our current home, despite the high rent.

This year I have finally seen that I no longer need to live this way. By learning to love me and see myself clearly for the first time, I am able to be confident in whom I am and the skills I have.

Finally, I have made a decision to earn what I know I am entitled to, based on the skills and qualifications I have. This is the turning point that will allow me to pay off my debts and begin to take me towards financial freedom, which is something I have been wanting for a long time.

My Story as I see it now

When I look back I can see that my language with money was set when I was young. No role models came into my life to teach me otherwise and so I simply accepted the boundaries set. Now that my awareness is more present, I have often listened to my parents saying how they cannot afford things or stating something is too expensive. This I now understand is their perception based on their understanding of their own circumstances. However, when hearing this language as a child it created boundaries and limitations as to what to expect.

If I apply the Law of Attraction to this way of thinking this vibration creates more of the same, never breaking free of the cycle until something in my awareness changes the perception.

By believing something is too expensive or that money is tight, this is the outcome that must be created in order to make the mind right.

Living within limitations has meant that even when money has come my way, it soon disappeared again.

Part of me carried a lot of guilt for disrupting my children's lives and not providing them with someone who would help to support, love and nurture them alongside me. Wanting to make up for the lack of interaction with grandparents and their own father, whenever I could I would treat them to little things in order to help ease the gap that I felt was there. At Christmas I would make a special effort to provide them with lots of presents so that they did not feel the lack that came from other people in their lives, as I saw it.

Now I can see that my focus on this lack simply created more of it. If I had let go of the concern and trusted that support and love would come, it would have allowed it in. By holding on to a thought that was negative, I ensured that a negative experience was encountered.

Credit cards became a simple option since they were easy to obtain at the time. Believing I could maintain the payments as I had savings back then I was happy using them. After a while of playing this game and juggling all I had, the debts grew bigger; my savings ran out leaving me with no option but to place each card into debt management. This was a difficult time, receiving calls and letters from those who I owed money to. However, having worked helping others with their debts through my financial work, it gave me the skills to deal with my own.

Ironically because this is what I had focused on within my job the idea in my mind had been set that this too could happen to me. By allowing in such thoughts I managed to create an outcome that matched.

When you focus on the lack of something it creates more lack. No matter how many things are going on around you, the energy of these thoughts is very powerful and will eventually become your reality.

At some point I could have chosen to go bankrupt, since this would have been an easy option given my circumstances. However, since I had acquired these debts I feel responsible to pay them back as best I can. My desire to do Estate Planning as part of my job and to be a Parent Governor at schools means bankruptcy is also not an option.

Maybe holding on to the debts has been part of my comfort zone, although not comfortable at all. Some might say it could be seen as self-sabotaging behaviour. By keeping them there in the background I am constantly reminded of my past. By not letting them go it becomes a punishment always present and a way of keeping my self esteem where I recognise it best.

My saving grace is I have always believed strongly that somehow I would pay them off and rise out of this dark place I have been in around money. Now this is becoming a reality and I can feel the changes within me allowing myself to finally create this outcome. By learning to love me I realise I no longer need to punish myself because of my beliefs in the past.

Now I can see that the lack of love for myself, the guilt that I was carrying for putting my children through so much upheaval and the previous conditioning I held around money were all factors in making it acceptable to live a limited life financially.

Now that my awareness is greater, I can also see looking back that I have often attracted boyfriends and friends who also had very little money - people who struggled with the same things as me. They were simply showing me what it looked like from outside of myself.

After reading Conversations with God by Neale Donald Walsh, I can see that each experience we have is directly reflecting back to us aspects of ourselves so that we can get to know ourselves better. We are each acting out who we believe ourselves to be and as a result are experiencing the consequences in return.

So if your task is to be loving and giving to others but you are not this to yourself, it is likely you will attract people who are takers and give nothing back.

The lesson thus being, you need to include yourself in your loving and giving behaviour. If however you are loving and giving to yourself your experiences with others will reflect this and you will be mingling with those who are the same.

If you have a low self-esteem, how could you attract someone who is confident? Someone who is confident is unlikely to understand your perception and more likely to be a constant reminder of your inadequacy. This is likely to make you feel uncomfortable and unless you are ready to change this, you will probably be more inclined to walk away from their friendship and love. Consequently you are more likely to feel comfortable with someone who feels the same. Together you will reflect aspects of this behaviour to each other, each experiencing what it is like to be this way. If you find yourself becoming annoyed by the other person it may be that you have reached a point when you wish to change.

Now, looking around at those I have attracted into my life and back towards myself, I can see that the changes I have been implementing into my life have brought me to a new awareness and perspective. They have helped me to see the old life for what it was and to begin to create a different one within a new reality.

Finally I am setting myself free from the past. As my business says I have been Aspiring 2 b free. This new freedom can be likened to starting a new novel - each page presently blank with the opportunity to be filled with new and exciting adventures.

If I do not wish the past to be repeated, the only way I can change my story is to change me.

Instead of being upset by my journey in life so far and holding regrets, I have learnt to see the gifts in the lessons taught to me along the way.

Like being at school, when I first began to read it felt difficult. As I progressed and began to enjoy my success the words flowed more freely and I could read whatever came my way. Soon I was able to appreciate the joy of reading and open my mind to new and exciting opportunities of learning. The same can be said of life.

Tools I have used to help me

Emotional Freedom Technique (EFT)

Since a lot of my thinking around money has been negative in the past, EFT has been a brilliant tool to help me overcome my challenges with it.

As my awareness has grown of my emotional self, I have been able to work with EFT to shift negative thoughts as they have arisen. This has helped me to redefine my thinking around money and given me a positive outlook instead.

For example, if you think about someone in debt, each time they go to the letterbox they begin to dread what letters will arrive. An ex boyfriend of mine used to go into a cold sweat each time he saw a brown envelope for that very reason.

His thoughts and feelings around the post eventually became very distorted. Since this was a daily occurrence for him, the negative energy was reinstalled every day.

This negative vibration soon became a reality and more debt and letters were created. As the debt increased his vibration became lower and the experiences that he received outside of this began to match this causing him one challenge after another in all areas of his life. He became very withdrawn and depressed as a result.

EFT can be likened to the fire brigade at this point. It helps to put out the fire and cool the energy down to a calm and more peaceful place.

Once in a calmer place it is good to look at the core reasons behind why the debt may have arisen in the first place. Usually this is due to a lack of self-esteem and self-love or a response to experiences the person has undergone that knocked their energy down at the time.

Once the core reason is established, EFT can be used to obliterate the effects of the memory and bring it to a place of acceptance and love. Once in acceptance and love the vibration shifts and the person releases it so that it no longer affects the way they think. Sometimes it can take several weeks of using EFT before the core reason will show itself. EFT will help to clear each layer as it is revealed through life experiences.

For my ex he needed to face himself. To see and accept the internal dialogue he had within himself before he could change the way he was behaving and the life he was creating as a result.

Meditation/Being in the NOW

The use of meditation in my life has helped to change my ability to become more aware of the reality of my situation.

When I first started doing meditation my mind would often be blocked with negative thoughts and feelings constantly bombarding me. My desire to face these and deal with them was not strong enough and so I felt it was better to ignore them and stop meditating.

After a while of more hurtful experiences and a stronger desire within me to change, I was able to embrace meditation differently and see the benefits of what it could bring.

This brought me to the spiritual awakening part of my life. The more my spirit awoke the greater the experience of life became. I was able to see things from a perspective that never would have occurred to me before. My mind became sharper as I let go of the rubbish it had been carrying and made room for new information to reside there.

By being still I was able to monitor my life in the present moment rather than reflecting on it after the event. By making this adjustment it allowed me to deal with experiences as they occurred rather than finding ways to overcome them later.

For example, by using **The Safety Zone** mentioned above, as a result of my new ability to be aware, I was able to see my children's behaviour as their own instead of making it personal to me. As I learnt to do this more, I was able to choose my responses more wisely instead of entering into the drama with them and acting like a hurt child too.

Working within **The Safety Zone** and with my chakras has helped to open my heart, be in acceptance of change and allow help and support from the universe and the earth to permit the life that I wish for to become my new reality.

Law of Attraction

Law of Attraction plays a big role in creating the experiences we have. It is a fundamental law that if unknown can leave you blindly entering into the same patterns of behaviour time and time again.

When I discovered the Law of Attraction it made so much sense of my life.

Often, despite wanting something to be different in your life, the fundamental thing that needs to change to achieve it is you.

To become aware of the aspect of you that needs to change, an experience has to be created that will help you to understand how. This could simply be someone explaining it to you. If you are in alignment with what is said, you will be in acceptance of the information given and make the changes suggested.

If however you are not quite in alignment yet, the words said will simply be words. Instead you will need to experience the consequences of this behaviour in a way that brings your awareness to it. This can sometimes mean having to go through a challenging event in order to finally feel it and see it for what it is.

When I say not in alignment, I mean that your mind is not quite ready to accept that the change mentioned is required to get what you want. By receiving the experience, it will help you to understand at a deeper level the meaning and consequences of this behaviour. The seed that has already been sown with words that may have been said to you will gain more clarity and you will gain insight into what needs to be done to positively change things. You still may not wish to address this at this time if it means letting go of relationships or changing your work. However, if you put your head in the sand another more challenging experience will come along in an attempt to deepen your insight even further.

For example, twice I have worked in the pub industry for extra cash and both times ended with some difficulty, the second time more challenging than the first. The second situation created was totally out of my control and very challenging, giving me no choice but to step away. At the time of working I remember having negative thoughts about the environment and feeling an outsider. This was subsequently created as a reality.

Having experienced the death of my brother through alcohol and my spiritual awakening since then, I now see that my higher self was steering me away from this type of work for a reason. Hindsight is a wonderful thing.

Another example I heard recently was to think of a Satnav in your car. When you first set off on your journey everything looks to be great. Then you hit a traffic jam or road works or worse still an accident. Sometimes you are forced to stop and other times you decide to take an alternate route. Despite the disruption eventually you find your way to the destination you chose.

This is just the same as applying the Law of Attraction. Your focus is on the destination. You may become distracted for a while, have to stop and think about a different way to do things or simply dig up some old hurts and heal them before finally reaching the place you want to be.

The more I learn to appreciate money the greater my experience becomes with it. As my focus shifts from negativity to positivity, as per the Law of Attraction, positive things begin to occur. Without first experiencing a lack of it, I may never have come to this realisation.

Appreciation

Appreciating and enjoying money changes my energy towards it. It lifts the feeling of limitation and replaces it with moments of feeling abundant. As a feeling of abundance becomes my focus the reality to match this begins to form. The difficulty has been to maintain this constantly if I wish my life to transform completely. This has taken a while, especially where my thoughts and feelings around money have been deeply engrained. Time and patience has been required to change my reality and is an on-going process.

Appreciation is a joyful energy that can be likened to a child laughing while swinging on a swing; the feeling of freedom and limitless possibilities that opens the heart to receive new things.

When your heart is open your vibration raises and the wishes that match this vibration manifest easily and quickly.

To manifest money means to know and believe you deserve it. When you appreciate the money you have it invites the universe to bring you more.

Often money is taken for granted when it arrives in your bank account. Taking the time to appreciate it and openly be grateful shows that you are aware of its existence. When you buy groceries or pay a bill being thankful that you can shows that you appreciate what you have.

When your vibration is low your focus stays in a negative place. Learning to bring appreciation into your day will help to raise your vibration and give you the positive focus you need to change what is your current mental state.

Money Biography

Whilst going through the process of change to become aware of my conscious thoughts around money, I listened to an expert in this field who suggested doing a Money Biography. This helped me to open my awareness to my thoughts around money.

A Money Biography is a journal of your relationship with money. To do yours, spend time writing out each period of your life in spaces of 10 years going back as far as you can remember.

Within each of these periods of time think about the influences that were around you with regards to your outlook on money. This will include people and experiences that you have encountered.

For example, from ages 0 - 10 include all those who took care of you during this time. If your time was spent with many different people your outlook may be varied. The experiences you received affecting the confidence in yourself and those of money will all have an impact on how you feel about it now.

Write out anything you can remember that was said to you about money and everything you can remember saying or feeling around money during each decade. Particularly note down any negative experiences you remember around finances and money whether yours or something you heard about from others around you. This may even be a world event or stock market crash that had an impact on those around you or which appeared on the news during that time period.

As you go through each of these decades you may notice a pattern that is repeating itself or a change after certain events have occurred.

Once you have completed it the results will show to you some of the reasons why money is either abundant or lacking or varied in your life.

After completing mine it was clear that my childhood and the negative impact upon my thinking with regards to myself were a big influence in how my journey unfolded.

Summary

Money is energy and so flows in the universe the same as you. If your vibration is low and you remain focussed on the lack of money, your flow of energy will become blocked and you will find yourself eventually in financial difficulty.

Becoming aware of your relationship with money will help you to understand more clearly the effects your thoughts are having on the flow of money into your life.

Keeping a daily record of money coming in and out of your day will help you to become focused upon it. The more you are aware of what is happening the easier it is to adjust any deficiencies or overspending. It is easy to put your head in the sand and hope that all will be well when you feel in fear deep within that it will not. This fear will keep your energy low and have an effect on what comes to you.

Appreciating every bit of money that comes your way will help to encourage the flow of more. What you focus on you create. By appreciating money you are bringing a good feeling vibration towards this experience and this will allow more such experiences to follow.

Adjusting your wealth thermometer will help you to overcome limited expectations around money. This thermometer within you will have been set when you were young.

Allow yourself to imagine a life where money is abundant. If you feel yourself doubting it, use EFT to help you tap away any limiting beliefs and thoughts.

Things you can do to help yourself

1. **Money Biography**

Spend time doing the money biography talked about above.

Once completed, taking each decade separately, look for any negative thoughts and feelings written and underline or highlight them.

Taking each decade separately, starting from when you were born, write out some statements that you can use with the EFT tapping. (See **Appendix 2** for help with how to use EFT)

Tap each statement out and if you feel you can add to it by remembering more to the memory around it, bring in different statements as you go around the set routine.

Keep doing this until you feel the memory is no longer having any emotional impact upon you. You will feel calm and peaceful around this if complete.

2. **Law of Attraction**

Looking back at your experiences with money in the biography, thinking of the Law of Attraction note down the thoughts that you feel may have led to these experiences.

Think of this like having a paintbrush in your hand and painting the experience as you think the thought. Sometimes, the thoughts you think may have created the experience may not be the ones that did.

However, by doing the exercise it will help you to become aware of what may have contributed to the outcome you received.

An example of thoughts that may have created something which you meant to have an alternative result are:

"I don't want to be in debt, I need money."

"I am fed up with never having money. I am going to get a job."

"I wish to be with a wealthy partner."

Each of these has a negative connotation, even though your intention was to get away from the problem. That is the problem. The very fact you are saying things to run away from the problem means you are not addressing the core reason the problem exists.

"I don't want to be in debt, I need money."

The focus is on the lack of money. This focus simply creates more of it. Instead you might want to say "At the moment I owe (put a figure in) amount of money. What is the best solution open to me to clear it?"

This way you are acknowledging the problem rather than pushing it away. It allows you to face it head on and see a solution from the positive outlook you now have.

"I am fed up with never having money. I am going to get a job."

Once again the focus is on the lack of money. The

vibration you are carrying at this point will be low and is unlikely to attract you to the type of job that will become the solution.

If instead you were to change your focus from the lack of money to attracting in a job you would love to do, the energy you would feel doing this would be far more positive. Consequently it has a greater likelihood of creating a more positive outcome.

Spend time looking at your skills and becoming excited by the prospect of a job, and notice your vibration change.

"I wish to be a with a wealthy partner."

A person may be wealthy but it does not mean they will be generous, loving or kind. Sometimes people can be very mean who are wealthy. If you genuinely wish to attract this type of partner be more specific about what you wish for. However, ensure that you yourself are also of a vibration that can match their qualities, for if you are not, they will soon see through you and move on to someone who is. Or alternatively, they may be extremely controlling and your lack of self worth and love may simply keep you limited under their rules.

3. **Being in the NOW**

To learn to be present it is important to practice being still with your mind.

Find half an hour when you know you are likely to be undisturbed. Write some time out in your diary if necessary. Find a quiet place to be, sit comfortably.

Taking a flower or a piece of fruit in your hand, practice simply looking at it. Keep your mind totally focused upon it. As you feel your thoughts drifting off to other things, draw yourself back to the object.

Look at it with no thoughts only an observation of all that it is. To begin with you may need to allow thoughts of the flower or fruit so that your mind becomes occupied with this object, forcing other thoughts away.

After a few times of practicing this, see if you can sit with a blank mind only observing the object.

When you can do this for five minutes you may like to practice doing this same exercise with no object. Instead close your eyes and focus only upon your breath.

The more practiced you are at being in the moment of now the easier it will become your normal state of being. As a result it will begin to change your life as you see the reality of now and become more connected to it.

4. **Abundance**

For one month, practice becoming aware of money coming to you and feeling appreciation for it. Notice yourself connecting to a sense of feeling abundant. Even small amounts can bring this feeling.

You could get yourself a Citrine crystal. (See **Appendix 5** - Crystals for more information). Hold this in your hand when thinking of the money that has come to you in the day. Thank the crystal for helping you with attracting it into your life.

Career/business

My Story as I saw it then

When I first set off from school with my qualifications in hand, I found it hard to imagine what job I would like to do.

At first I went away to university to study a BSC in Catering and Applied Nutrition but realised early on it wasn't for me. Two terms later I returned home.

After a year of doing a secretarial course I began working in accounts for a dry cleaning company. A year later the office announced they were relocating to Milton Keynes so I decided to move jobs to work for a solicitor doing wills and probate.

Whilst working in the solicitors I decided Law would be a great degree to do and began a 4-year course, whilst continuing to work full time.

A year later my old company came back to the Midlands and asked for me to join their Pensions Department, agreeing to fund my degree. A few years later in the final year of my degree I fell pregnant and left. A short while later, this company was bought out by a larger dry cleaning firm when their stock price plummeted.

Whilst my children were small I looked for jobs that allowed me to stay at home with them, varying between selling books and cosmetics, doing accounts for a local firm, working in as a barmaid and telesales.

When the children were all at school I went to work fulltime taking a role as an HR Assistant in an automotive factory. During this time I attended College to gain a qualification for this. It taught me lots and after three years I was made redundant.

At this point I decided to move down South with my children and was offered a job selling mortgages. My previous firm offered me the opportunity to stay in the Midlands when the HR Manager handed in her notice but it was too late, I had already decided to move.

It took me four months to do my mortgage exams whilst learning on the job. My first post was working within an estate agent, which led to a change a year later to work for another helping them to set up their own mortgage advising firm. After another year I decided to become self-employed.

The mortgage crash came quickly after. Using my law knowledge it seemed a good fit to switch to estate planning, advising clients on their last will and testaments. This was enjoyable at first but my spiritual business Aspire2bfree was becoming my passion and so I devoted more and more time to this.

As I began to develop spiritually and learn to connect to my inner sanctuary, my business evolved along with me. It led me to running events, channeling e-books, running workshops, holding one to one sessions and running groups to share the knowledge I had learnt and was learning.

Each experience led me towards opening my creative self further until finally I wrote and published a children's book, of which there are to be 9 more in the series. I also felt a strong urge to finish a thriller I had been writing for years.

Now I am writing my story, Standing Tall, which encapsulates most of what I have learned so far.

Throughout my time in self-employment, especially during the last few years, many have urged me to stay focused on one thing and make a success of this.

I have listened and tried to follow what they say, but my own inner self has different ideas. It can see a vision of three very different types of books fitting together to form one message for all. This is a concept not many book agents would be comfortable with and so to follow my heart it has meant self-publishing my books.

This divergence of energies has meant that financial reward has been slow in coming. This could be seen as a way of self-sabotaging or instead a passion that is so strong only by following it will it truly be fulfilled.

My Story as I see it now

My auntie recently said to me that she feels "I have wasted my intelligence" by not heading into a career, based on the fact that I am highly qualified with a degree in Law and with many other qualifications since.

Some may agree looking back at my career and seeing the constant chopping and changing that has gone on.

However, I am now in a place of understanding myself much clearer than ever before. Without this journey of varied experiences I might never have had the time or confidence to explore my creative talents as much as I have.

Creativity is love - by loving who you are it allows your true essence to flow. The more that I have moved away from traditional structure, the freer I have become to unlock my own potential.

It is true I could have made things easier for myself by sticking to one career but then what would I have learnt. My life would have become comfortable and structured and as a result stagnant. It would not have given me the same urges to change since once successful in something the desire is usually to keep building on that success.

My observation during my journey of change is that we live in a very structured world. The expectations given to us by our parents and school are to find a career and stick with it. However, as a child it is unlikely that you will know yourself well enough to know the truth of who you are unless you have been lucky enough to have parents who have encouraged this.

Living with a sense of uncertainty has given me the opportunity to explore new ideas and to get to know myself more deeply. Learning to love me has added to this and given me a greater chance of doing work that I love to do.

The greatest success you can have in a career is to truly love what you do and not see it as a job at all, earning enough to satisfy your needs or requirements.

When I was a teenager my careers adviser asked me what I wanted to do. My answer was, to be a ventriloquist. Funny how things work out! In my mind then it meant sitting with a dummy on my knee and pretending to speak on its behalf. The reality of now is through my books and channeling I am a different kind of ventriloquist working with angels, spirit guides, ascended masters and my own higher self.

Through observation I have come to realise that the universe is an amazing place. As we have thoughts and feelings, these create an outcome. These outcomes lead us to people and places often giving us the answers we need to move forward in our lives.

When you truly let go and stop worrying about the future it frees you up to explore life to the full now. The future for my brother never came and this is the same for many. We cannot say how many days we will live or how many places we will go. We can only appreciate today and all that it brings and take steps towards creating the future we desire, even if we never get there. By enjoying and appreciating each day it allows you to enjoy the journey, so no matter whether you get there or not, you will have been happy stepping towards it.

If it is for the greater good of all, it is likely your work will continue even when you are gone. By letting go of the need to control when and how you can focus on now and make today fun.

At one point I thought perhaps I had a problem in learning to commit yet when I consider my commitment to my children, I now know this not to be true. I thought perhaps I was self-sabotaging and destroying any chances of success by spreading myself thinly. Now I can see I was simply exploring. My adventure led me to learn much about business, people and the effects of not loving the self.

Often we look for reasons to pin our lack of fulfilling expectations upon, judging ourselves to help us justify the circumstances we are in. Yet I now realise it simply does not matter. Whatever the reasons, today is all that counts.

Today I have a vision of what I wish my life to be and the work I want to do. Each loving step that I take towards it right now leads me closer to achieving my dream. Each day that I let go of the fear of what will be, I set myself free to see what is and enjoy what comes.

Tools I have used to help me

Creativity

The greatest gift my journey has given me is the ability to be confident in myself which in turn has helped my creativity to flow.

Creativity has helped me to trust in who I am and what I am able to do. Each of us is a natural creator. Our whole lives are spent creating from the thoughts and feelings that we have.

Without creativity nothing would change. The world would simply stop. Creativity is therefore life itself. It is the very thing that keeps the flow of the world moving.

Creativity from a place of love brings with it a pure vibration. Its very essence will only create that which is of a loving purpose to the consciousness as a whole.

When your heart is opened wide it reveals gifts that reside within you that otherwise you would not have discovered.

When you are suppressed and hidden behind the veils of your conditioning your life is run on automatic pilot. Each thing that you do lacks the presence of love in an unconditional form. Instead your mind is preoccupied by the recordings of the past and those around you causing you to act from this.

By learning to connect within myself, it has given me access to a new energy - one that is full of joy and passion for what I do.

Creativity has helped me to see through my past and given me the opportunity to be vulnerable again without the fear of being hurt. The effects of my childhood no longer provide a shroud over me but instead give me a platform to create from.

Creativity can come in many forms, some of which are not obvious - for example, think of a food that you like - I choose olives - many people have invented flavourings in order to entice you to eat them - each person has done this through their own interpretation of something within them - so many ways today you can now eat an olive!!

Creativity is about having fun - exploring your childlike innocent self and loving every minute doing it. Being creative will automatically shift any negative energies you may be feeling and help you to open your heart to loving feelings instead.

Watching television is a distraction from life - developing what is to be on television is creativity. Sometimes you might welcome distractions, but if the majority of the time you can be creative, think how much richer your life would be.

Creativity has opened up new and endless possibilities within my career and business making it exciting and enjoyable. There is never time to become bored or complacent with it.

For me the joy of making something from nothing that will lovingly help others is the greatest gift of life there can be.

Self Love

If you are in business or a career while lacking love for yourself, the chances are your mind is likely to be filled with judgment and expectations both of yourself and others. This may often cause you disappointment and hurt when you or others don't perform as well as you hope.

Without love for the self it is likely that what drives you is either money or the need to serve others to gain some kind of self worth and value. Your belief in yourself may be low and your need to succeed high.

When disconnected to such love within me, I was left floating from job to job exploring who I was and what I wanted for myself. Always eager to please and needing to feel appreciation from others I can now see was a reflection of what I lacked for myself.

Learning to love me has taught me to be truthful to myself and not to be led into things by the wishes of others. It has given me my power back, reignited a flame within and drawn me to the passion of what I love to do.

As this energy builds I feel more joy in my life that leads me to appreciate others and myself too. As I appreciate others opportunities begin to open and I feel confident to explore them. As I trust myself it allows me to trust others, allowing in much needed help and support that before I had always shunned away with the very thoughts I was having.

Instead of the darkness that I once felt, the whole of me feels lighter and brighter and as a result the work that I do carries with it this essence too.

Understanding what brings me Joy

The energy of joy is one of the highest vibrations there is. It brings with it abundance, gratitude, peace within and a sense of fulfilment.

To reach this is to know thy self truly. To have peeled back the onion as they say and revealed the core of whom you are.

This requires time and patience. Each day is a chance to connect to the love you hold within. As you connect to love you engage the source of knowledge that is personal to you. Think of it like searching the hard drive of a computer and finding all the original files that were there before you began downloading things onto it.

One way to find out what would bring you joy is to focus upon it. Every morning ask yourself what will bring me joy today? Allow yourself to experience moments of it, doing things that you love. This could even be as simple as meditating, having a cup of tea or even stroking a cat. Joy is not about being ecstatic for this energy is the opposite of feeling really sad and eventually you will have to come down from it.

Joy is a sense of feeling balanced, of feeling love and peace within you and with others. The more you can sustain this the easier it will be to deal with all aspects of life.

Practice having one day to yourself where you dedicate it entirely to you, doing only the things you love to do. As you go through your day notice which things genuinely bring you to a place of feeling joy and contentment. What makes your face smile and your heart sing?

Once in a state of joy it is the best time to manifest things into your life. Spend some time writing out your dreams and desires. Close your eyes and imagine them taking place. This is particularly good if you have a vision for your business or career ahead. By writing out your ideas whilst in this energy you will bring positive energy to it, consequently drawing ideas that come from this same state.

Vision Board

As discussed earlier in the book, the Law of Attraction governs what you manifest. If your focus is drawn towards the positive things you wish to manifest, it will be more helpful to your thought processes.

A vision board will help you to achieve this. It can simply be a piece of paper or an actual board or even a scrapbook that you look at often.

Taking any of these, on the blank space put pictures, words and sentences of things you would like to bring into your life. These can be anything you choose. As this section is about business and career, focus on this. What type of work would you like to do? What sort of people would you like to work with? How do you wish to feel when you are doing it? What income would you like to earn? Where do you wish to work? Use pictures and words to put answers to these questions and others you may like to ask into a visual format.

Place the vision board somewhere that will come into your peripheral view from time to time. If in a scrapbook, ensure that you take it out often or leave it lying somewhere that feels comfortable and is easy to view. If after a while you wish to change anything, remove pictures or words or simply add some.

Defining my Market

As an owner of my own business it has been important to understand who my audience is. If my message is too broad it is like placing leaves into the ocean - they simply become insignificant and are washed away.

For my message to have any impact I have realised it must have an audience to reach. For example, if I were selling an energy drink I would need to think about what sort of person would want to purchase such a drink. What benefits would it give to them?

Since opening my business Aspire2bfree in 2011 it has been a journey of discovery. Understanding myself first before knowing whom my real audience is to be. Having been able to help those who have searched for me or have been recommended to me it has given me experiences to help me understand more clearly whom I want to work with. To bring out my best potential, I have had to learn which parts bring out my passion and fulfil me.

If you are looking to succeed in a business or career, it is important first to understand who you want to spend time helping or working with. Knowing your own values and understanding your skills and appreciating them will help you to define this.

It seems a simple thing yet many find it difficult to do since they are in fear of missing others who might also benefit from what they do, know or sell. However, it is not possible to help or sell to everyone. All people are unique and special in their own right. The journey of one person may not inspire someone who has been on a totally different one. They may need to hear words from the person who understands them because of what they have been through. By knowing yourself you can identify whom you can help the most.

For example, it is no good trying to sell tampons to a man. They have no use for them. Alternatively it is useless selling cufflinks to women - unless they are in fancy dress. The only exception to both of these is where someone is in the wrong body or feels uncomfortable being their own sex, for they may wish to cross dress or undergo surgery.

For those with a message to share, although the teachings you have to offer can be used for many circumstances, the way they are expressed and the examples given are the potion to healing the wounds.

Only those who are open to such a potion will be willing to use it.

Letting go and Adapting to Change

As part of my journey change has been at every corner calling me. Moving from one thing to the next I have constantly been learning and developing something new.

We live in times of change. If you look back only 500 years ago you will see how much change mankind has endured.

Yet still as humans we fear change. We like the idea of being settled and having structure within our lives. It gives us a sense of peace and the idea that we are successful in some way.

Without change the world would remain the same and this is impossible. Nature shows us that change is inevitable. Everything is given the opportunity to grow and flourish. Sometimes things happen that prevent this and things perish before they have the chance to. Other times they grow and perish on the way. Nothing in life is permanent. Everything alters in some way each day, even if only slightly. Even mountains that seem to be static alter and shift with the weather and the underground current of the earth.

I remember once spending time in a garden watching a mushroom blossom and glow in the sunshine over several days then witnessing it wizen and die as its time had come to an end.

By accepting that change is inevitable, that each day you live new things are possible, you can open your life and expand what is in your current consciousness. By expanding your awareness you can begin to create greater and more meaningful things in your life, letting old and negative ways gradually disappear.

When you have acceptance that nothing is permanent, that at some point all things begin and end, you can learn to let go of expectations and allow everything to just be as it is.

Practice saying to yourself,, '*All is in divine order. Everything is as it is meant to be in this moment of time.*'

The more you say it the easier it will be to believe it. As you believe it you begin to live it as it aligns with your vibration and beliefs.

Letting go of the fear of change and allowing all things possible will open up an amazing unlimited life for you. You are the captain of your ship. You have the ability and power to be whoever you want to be. Even if it seems impossible, by believing in miracles and letting go of limited thoughts, it allows unlimited solutions to show themselves that may not have been in your consciousness before.

Think back to me wanting to be a Ventriloquist - the meaning of this can be taken in many ways. The resulting idea of what I do today never entered my mind. Everything you say, think and do is the same. By permitting yourself to be open to all that the universe presents to you, based on what is best for you and the good of all, will help contribute to a more loving experience for you and those you connect with in the world.

It is good to remember we are all one consciousness. As one consciousness whatever you bring into your awareness you are bringing into the awareness of all. You are creating it and making it possible. Others are simply responding to it and creating their own set of circumstances and experiences as a result.

Summary

Understanding yourself from a deeper perspective will help guide you towards a career that will bring you fulfilment.

Allowing yourself to embrace change will help you to discover different aspects of yourself that will enhance your abilities. This will open the doors to new opportunities, ones that before you would never have considered.

If you are choosing to become self employed, focus on whom your audience is. The more closely you define it, the easier it will be to market what you choose to offer to them.

Monitor your feelings around success. What are your visions of this? If you notice them to be limited, ask yourself why. Focusing on this, work with EFT to help you eliminate any negative beliefs and thoughts that may hold you back.

Creativity can help to open your inner flow, connecting you to ideas that are likely to increase your fulfilment at work. This can include activities such as writing, drawing, painting, model making, baking - anything where you are creating something from scratch.

Visualising what you want in a career or business can help draw your focus to the solutions you need in creating it. Vision boards are a great way of achieving this since they focus your attention on the details and remind you daily, as you observe them, what it is you desire.

Things you can do to help yourself

1. **Defining whom to work with**

Spend time writing out what is important to you business wise. What type of clients/customers would you like to work with? Or what type of product would excite you and be easy to sell? Or what are your passions? - The things you love doing the most. How could this be created into a business? What have you become an expert in that you could share with others? What benefits could you offer to others that they would be willing to pay for? There are so many questions you could ask - this is your journey. Add more in and be as specific as you can so that you define what is truly right for you.

For example, it may be that you love travelling. If this was to be your job, what aspect of it could you do that will create an income enough to allow you to do it full time.

If you find yourself limiting your answers by adding buts and maybes, spend some time doing some EFT to clear these thoughts. The freer you are with your choices here the more likely you will be ready to explore them further and take them to the next stage.

2. **Vision Board**

Once you have looked at what you want to do and with whom, create a vision board to match. Details of how are given in the vision board section above.

It may be that you are simply revamping what you already do. This too can be included on a vision board. The more specific you are the easier it will be for the universe to work with you to help bring your awareness to the pathway to it.

3. **Letting Go of your Story**

To help you understand yourself better write out your story in stages of 10 years, e.g. 0-10 11-20 etc. Split the page into two columns. Label one side the good things and the other, the challenging things. As you see your story evolve you will witness whether your life has been balanced or if it sways more to one column or the other.

As you write the story at the end of each decade ask yourself if you were happy or sad during it.

When you have completed it, with the knowledge you have today rewrite how you might have done something different using the data from one of the challenging times. What perspective can you see today that you couldn't see then? As you do this you will see how much you have changed. This will allow you to see the benefits of your journey and what you have become an expert in.

If you cannot see a different perspective and feel you would do things the same, use EFT to help you release any challenging and emotional feelings around it. Ask yourself if there is any forgiveness that you could do for yourself or others included within it which would help release emotional blocks from this experience.

To Conclude

Each person is uniquely on their own journey, exploring who they are as part of this world. Every relationship and experience comes as a result of this, creating circumstances that bring learning giving all involved an opportunity to develop and grow.

Every step of the journey is important and adds value to the learning given even if it does not feel that way at the time.

When you consider you are creating with your thoughts and feelings as part of one consciousness it is easier to see why being aware of what you communicate as part of this is important. When you are conscious of your thoughts and feelings it gives you greater opportunity to have an impact on the world from a perspective that you would desire rather than one that has been taught to you.

For example, if the universe were a cow, what impact would your current thoughts and behaviours be having on the cow? Are you happy with this? If not, what could you begin to do differently that would change this view?

How you live your life is totally your own choice. You can decide to experience any aspect of the world in whatever way you choose. However, when you are aware of your choices you become aware that they are also having an impact on others and on the future of those yet to come.

For example, most people know that alcohol is toxic and a poison to the body. Those that choose to drink it are doing so because they wish to experience something from it. Sometimes the experience can lead to violence towards another or reckless behaviour despite that not being the person's intention.

Once hooked to the experience of alcohol it can be very difficult to break the habit despite knowing and seeing the consequences of continuing to drink it. It is only when an experience comes as a result of it that affects the person directly or they witness the effects on another that it may enter their consciousness to change.

If it is only their own health that is suffering and they lack self-love, it is unlikely they will see a good enough reason to change unless something in their blueprint persists on pulling them back onto a different pathway.

There are no wrong or right ways to live your life. There is no one judging you except yourself. God/your inner sanctuary does not judge you. God/your inner sanctuary merely guides you to the evidence of the consequences your choices result in through the life that is presented to you. You are the one creating the outcome through the way you respond.

For example, on entering the local dry cleaners I was offered a carrier bag. Thanking the man I said no. When I explained I was doing my bit to look after the environment, he said, "Why bother, it won't affect you?" This shocked me. His consciousness could not think beyond his own life. Mine was thinking of the future inhabitants of the earth and of the damage we are doing now to the planet that will affect them.

This difference in consciousness is experienced many times by many people. It is these differences that can cause ripples of positive change as ideas and thoughts are exchanged if directed in a focused and positive way.

When faced with challenging circumstances it is often an alarm bell that something within you is being called upon to change. Your outlook on life through your mind is directing these experiences towards you so that you can see yourself more clearly.

If you block these experiences by distracting yourself away from them, they will keep re-emerging into your life in different forms until you listen and take time to consider how you can change you. Some people may choose to become reclusive in order to avoid such confrontations, the fear of being hurt so strong within them that it limits their life completely. Whatever your choice, it is your life - the consequences you receive are merely a reflection of how you choose to be.

If you choose to connect to your heart, the experiences you receive will be drawn from a place of love. The more you express love, the greater love will become in what you experience.

Growing up around depression can leave long lasting effects if your awareness of these effects is limited or non-existent. Only when you begin to explore yourself and choose to change this can you begin to free yourself from the boundaries set by your experiences so far.

So many people these days are affected by depression because of the limited way we live our lives. From the day we are born we are subjected to the ideals of others until one day we have the courage to follow our own. For some that can be whilst young but for many it can take years for this to come.

Your body is made of energy. Everything you subject it to is granting your energy an experience. The food you eat and the fluid you drink each have qualities that will provide the body with the consequences that follow.

For example, if you put diesel into an unleaded vehicle it would immediately damage the engine. Your body is much cleverer than a vehicle because it is alive and wants to survive. It uses what you give it to create energy and to keep all your systems going.

However, after a long period of time of feeding it with the wrong types of fuel that have no healthy benefit, illnesses form as a result of the negative energy that has stored up. Sometimes these can be fatal if the abuse is consistently brutal and toxic. Food and drink can therefore eventually have the same negative impact as narcotics on the body if taken for long enough.

Every wave of thought that enters your mind carries a vibration. When you watch films or play games on a screen with murder and darkness within, these vibrations are interacting with you. The more you subject yourself to these kinds of vibrations the more negative your energy will become unless you have learnt how to clear it. Your mind may begin to create stories within your own life that will bring fear where otherwise it may not. It will draw you towards the foods that match this energy.

You may eventually become depressed, anxious, angry and frustrated as nothing you are doing is feeding the love you hold within. As nothing is feeding the love, joy and peace cannot find its way to the surface and bring you harmony in your life.

If you limit these experiences and fill your life with loving energies instead, eventually your energy will respond to this. The food you choose will become healthier; your choices will become more loving and your circumstances more abundant and joyful as a result.

Watching films that make you laugh, that are loving and have happy endings will fill your heart with joy. This joy will spread into the things you choose to do immediately after. If that is with others, they too will benefit from the joy and love will spread.

If instead they bring up sadness because they remind you of what you lack in your life, spend some time working on this sadness with EFT. Alternatively you could look inside yourself and see what needs to change so that you can be happy for others as well as yourself. How could you love yourself more so that you no longer feel as if love is missing?

Whatever your stage of understanding and learning is within this lifetime it will create the circumstances for others to learn too. Therefore nothing you do within your life will ever be a mistake. It will always provide education for the consciousness as a whole and for you. Everything is therefore always in perfect divine order.

It is more probable than not that you will at times do things from old habits when you hoped you would not. Each day is another opportunity to learn from the last and realign your thoughts to how you wish to be. The trick is not to judge yourself when you do but to accept and love yourself instead. You are a human being learning to love - the more you practice loving thoughts the greater chance you will have of truly feeling it and being it.

To help you achieve this, think of three words that describe you as you wish to be and recite them to yourself often. The more often you hear these words your mind will come to believe them and your actions will respond accordingly.

Aspiring to be free of the past and recreating a new outlook is the first step towards freeing yourself of a life you no longer want and bringing yourself into one you do.

A spiritual awakening is not about suddenly becoming aware of everything in your consciousness. It mostly happens gradually through experiences and events that change your perception, opening your mind to new information and possibilities.

This can take years since there will often be days when the old programming slips back into play unobserved. Only when something happens to re-alert you, will you become conscious again to change it.

Life is filled with opportunities to observe the information you receive daily and subsequently learn to apply it to situations personal to you. The more you practice allowing these insights into your awareness and action them, the deeper your connection will become to love - your inner sanctuary/God.

There is no race to see who is the most enlightened by the end of this lifetime.

You are on your own personal journey. How much you want to experience and endure during this lifetime is totally your choice. Once you are aware of this choice it becomes easier to steer your mind towards a more loving existence.

Thankfully I have chosen to listen to my inner sanctuary and make changes in my life that have brought me deeper loving relationships with my friends and family for which I am very grateful. As I have changed those around me have begun to change their perception of me, bringing a deeper love and greater harmony between us.

You too have the opportunity to change that which you are not happy with.

Your life is in your hands - be confident in loving you and the rest will follow.

Be patient and consistent in the changes you make. Let go of limiting thoughts and feelings as you observe them. Learn to love you so that you can love all and experience the world from a deeper more meaningful perspective. Visualise the life you want and create steps towards it, allowing the universe to guide you. Accept that nothing in life is permanent and watch your life transform.

Your past does not have to equal your future. It's your life to do with as you please.

It has been said that those who focus on the past become depressed and those who focus on the future become anxious and frustrated. The moral therefore is to focus on the NOW for this is where you will find your happiness.

You can either welcome change or choose to hate it. The choice is yours. If you choose to embrace change, take a small step today to begin making a positive difference in your life. You will be glad you did.

THE END

APPENDICES

Appendix 1 - Meditation and Mindfulness

Different Ways to Meditate

Meditation is a way of focusing your thoughts and improving your awareness of what you are thinking and feeling in any one moment.

By becoming more aware of what you are focusing on, it will naturally give you the opportunity to improve your life.

Often thoughts of a negative nature go undetected and as a result your life becomes a series of circumstances created as a result. Using meditation you can improve your awareness of such thoughts so that you can begin to readjust them accordingly, creating more positive outcomes.

Used on a daily basis, meditation can give you the opportunity to have a more focused and energised life.

Meditation - Focus on the Breath

To increase your awareness first you must become alerted to what is happening in your mind.

Meditation is a technique that involves bringing the mind to one single point of focus.

First you will need to find a comfortable place to sit. This can either be in a chair or on the floor. If on the floor, you might need some cushions around you to help support you if sitting for a long time, especially if you are not used to it. Usually the Lotus

Yoga position is chosen for this - sitting cross legged on the floor, with your back straight and your hands either resting on your knees or in your lap. You can look on the Internet for ways to do this.

If sitting on a chair, you can either have your feet touching the floor or on the chair sitting cross-legged. You may wish to support yourself with cushions, especially under your knees. The main thing is not to rest your head on the back of the chair since this could lead you to falling asleep whilst in a relaxed state of mind.

Once sitting comfortably, close your eyes. Begin to focus on your breath. Notice your breath as it goes in and out of the body.

As you focus on your breath thoughts will come into your mind. Be aware of them and let them go. You might like to see them as clouds forming in a blue sky, floating on by.

As these thoughts keep coming stay focused on your breath. If it helps, say in and out to yourself as the breath moves in and out.

At first 5 to 10 minutes of this is likely to be enough for you. After a while of practising, you may find that you can extend this time until eventually you can sit for 1 hour.

If you find focusing on your breath too difficult, try staring into a flame or at a flower or object chosen of your choice.

The idea is to keep your mind focused in one place allowing other thoughts to be acknowledged but with no attention paid to them.

This enables you to become aware of the thoughts you are having at the same time as not becoming absorbed by them. You are creating a bypass so that they can no longer distract you.

Below is a link to a short meditation to help you with focusing on the breath:

https://tinyurl.com/y9vdltbd

The more you practice meditation the easier you will find this and notice also the effects creeping into your every day life. Over time your general concentration will improve and you will find yourself being distracted less easily.

As you become aware of the thoughts you are having it will help you to understand some of the circumstances that are being created in your life right now. By recognising your thoughts you are becoming present. When you are present you are fully aware of what you are creating with the thoughts you are having. This gives you the power to change unwanted and unhelpful thoughts into something more in line with what you want to achieve.

Mindfulness Meditation

Mindfulness meditation is allowing you to take a deeper look at your life and body and see the reality of it.

You can practice this by sitting comfortably as before and closing your eyes.

Become aware of your breath. Begin to take your focus to different parts of the body. As you do, become aware of the sensations in that part of the body. Notice anything that feels uncomfortable or particularly good. Observe the feelings and allow the mind to walk on by.

As you observe you become aware of the sensations without getting involved in the details of them. This can be particularly useful when observing pain. Nothing in the body stays there permanently. All sensations come and go. If you are patient and keep observing the sensation eventually it will shift and go. Sometimes with this will come through thoughts that will bring your awareness to what may have caused it to reside there in the first place.

Mindful observations of the body will show you the reality of what is happening within. The more connected to your body and what is happening, the greater your connection will be to other things in your life.

For many life has become a habit - something you do simply because this morning you woke up. Looking deeper into your life will give you the opportunity to decide whether you like it or wish to change it. The deeper you look, the greater the healing that can arise and the more of your potential you will unlock.

Other Meditation Techniques

There are various other meditation techniques. Finding one that suits you will mean you are more likely to stick with it.

Some Buddhist monks focus directly on the cultivation of compassion. This involves visualising negative events and reframing them in a positive light by transforming them through compassion.

There are also moving meditations techniques, such as Tai Chi, Chi Kung and walking meditation.

You can try a walking meditation when you next go out into nature. Whilst you are walking become aware of your breath. Notice your breath and become present in the moment. The more present you become the greater your experience will be. It will enhance your connection to everything that is happening around you, helping you to enjoy being outdoors even more.

There are also Buddhists who chant. There are many different types of Buddhists, each with their own way of carrying out a daily practice of connecting to their inner self. Some who chant, simply have one mantra that they chant over and over again. They believe the words that they use carry with them a certain vibration that helps them to clear away any negative vibrations that they may be carrying. As they chant they will often get answers come into their minds in reply to a question they may be thinking about. Since their mind is distracted with the chant the answer is believed to be coming from the inner self, giving them the guidance they need to resolve the issue they have.

Benefits of Meditation

When using any form of meditation your body and mind become relaxed. As a result, regular use of meditation can sometimes:

- Benefit the nervous system:
- Lower blood pressure;
- Improve blood circulation;
- Lower heart rate; lessen perspiration;
- Slow your respiratory rate; lessen anxiety;
- Lower blood Cortisol levels;
- Give feelings of a healthier wellbeing;
- Help create less stress;
- Give deeper relaxation

The main goal of meditation is to be present. These benefits are possible outcomes as a result of it but not the main purpose behind it.

By becoming present your ability to function within your life will naturally improve. It will give you an awareness of things that previously you took for granted. By changing your awareness it gives you the opportunity to add improvements to your life that will benefit not only you but also those around you.

In Buddhist philosophy, the ultimate benefit of meditation is liberation of the mind from attachment to things it cannot control, such as external circumstances or strong internal emotions. Someone who practices meditation regularly learns to become calmer in their approach to life, allowing them to be a more balanced and rational human being. Their previous emotional self no longer leads the way but instead they gain a deeper understanding of situations that occur around them helping them to accept them more freely.

As their outlook and understanding changes, so does their response to life.

Appendix 2 - The Basics of Emotional Freedom Technique

EFT was first created by Gary Craig as a way of releasing negative emotional responses that have become lodged within the energetic body causing negative responses such as pain, illness, phobias, low self-esteem, fear, etc. His official website is: **https://www.emofree.com** where you will find lots of free resources and advice to help you.

Below I have written out an overview of the basics of EFT to introduce you to it so that you can consider it and practice with it, based on my experience with it as an EFT Practitioner. However, if you want to learn it in detail or train in this or work on other people using it, it is important to consult Gary's website or with a registered practicing EFT practitioner for professional tips and advice.

Below is the shortened version of EFT, which is suitable for most problems. For deeper traumas see further down for the extended version.

Getting Ready

It is important to prepare yourself before beginning to tap so that you get the most from the process. Negative thinking within the subconscious mind can sometimes get in the way. The statements are written in a way that counteracts this ensuring its effectiveness.

Connecting with the Problem

To get a direct result, first you must come up with a statement that describes the problem, e.g. I am frightened of spiders.

Speaking this out loud will help to engage your mind more clearly.

Think about the problem that you have. It could be a pain, a fear, a craving, an illness or perhaps a phobia, It is likely to be something that always makes you emotionally upset when you think about it. Be sure that you want to be rid of this feeling forever.

Create a statement that best describes the problem. The more specific you are the greater the effect it will have.

Creating the Statement

The EFT statement gives you the chance to acknowledge the problem and accept yourself anyway, despite the existence of the problem. This removes anything hiding in your subconscious mind.

The statement consists of the problem followed by a balancing statement or affirmation. The default affirmation in the statement is,

"I deeply and completely accept myself"

Here is an example:

You repeat the EFT statement 3 times:

Even though I have this (describe the problem), I deeply and completely accept myself.

A problem can be a worry, a feeling, a fear, or any other negative emotion.

Here are some examples.

- *Even though I have this* headache, *I deeply and completely accept myself.*
- *Even though I have this* stiffness in my neck, *I deeply and completely accept myself.*
- *Even though I have this* craving for alcohol, *I deeply and completely accept myself.*
- *Even though I have this* depression, *I deeply and completely accept myself.*

For my use I have added in the word love to give a deeper connection to the statement. The statement for me is:

Even though *I have (this problem),* I deeply and completely love and accept myself.

Some interesting points about the EFT set up:

It doesn't matter whether you love and accept you by saying it you are affirming it to your sub conscious mind.

For quicker results say it out loud. However, if your intention is strong and circumstances prevent you saying it out loud, saying it silently to yourself is just as good but the results may take a little longer.

Sore point and Karate chop

To enhance the effectiveness of the tapping you can rub the sore spot or tap on the Karate chop.

There are two Sore Spots both are just as effective. They are located in the upper left and right portions of the chest and you will find them as follows:

Go to the base of the throat about where you imagine a man to knot his tie. Find the U shaped notch at the top of your sternum (breastbone). From the top of that notch go down 3 inches toward your navel and over 3 inches to your left (or right). You should now be in the upper left (or right) portion of your chest. If you press carefully in that area (within a 2 inch radius) you will find a "Sore Spot." This is the place you will need to rub while saying the affirmation. This spot is sore when you rub it because lymphatic congestion occurs there. When you rub it, you are dispersing that congestion. Fortunately, after a few episodes the congestion is all dispersed and the soreness goes away. Then you can rub it with no discomfort whatsoever.

The Karate Chop point (abbreviated KC) is located at the centre of the fleshy part of the outside of your hand (either hand) between the top of the wrist and the base of the little finger or the part of your hand you would use to deliver a karate chop. Instead of rubbing it, tap the Karate Chop point with the fingertips of the index finger and middle finger of the other hand.

Using your statement and either the sore spots or the karate chop as described above, you can repeat the statement out loud 3 times. This will help to set the statement up ready for the full tapping sequence below.

The Tapping Sequence

By tapping on Meriden points, like those used in acupuncture, you can release the negative energy behind the statement being said.

Tapping Instructions:

You can tap with either hand but it is usually more convenient to do so with your dominant hand (e.g. right hand if you are right handed).

Tap with the fingertips of your index finger and middle finger. This covers a little larger area than just tapping with one fingertip and allows you to cover the tapping points more easily.

Tap solidly but never so hard as to hurt or bruise yourself.

Tap approximately 7 times on each of the tapping points or whatever feels comfortable.

Tapping Points

Below are the Meriden points set out in the order you would use them with a diagram to help:

Karate Chop: It is located in the middle of the fleshy part on the outside of the hand between the top of the wrist bone and the base of the little finger. It is abbreviated **KC**

Eyebrow Point: At the beginning of the eyebrow, just above and to one side of the nose. This point is abbreviated **EB**

Side of the Eye: On the bone bordering the outside corner of the eye. This point is abbreviated **SE**

Under the Eye: On the bone under an eye about 1 inch below your pupil. This point is abbreviated **UE**

Under the Nose: On the small area between the bottom of your nose and the top of your upper lip. This point is abbreviated **UN**

Chin: Midway between the point of your chin and the bottom of your lower lip. This point is abbreviated **CH**

Collar Bone: The junction where the sternum (breastbone), collarbone and the first rib meet. To locate it, first place your forefinger on the U-shaped notch at the top of the breastbone (about where a man would knot his tie). From the bottom of the U, move your forefinger down toward the navel 1 inch and then go to the left (or right) 1 inch. This point is abbreviated **CB**

Under the Arm: On the side of the body, it is about four inches below the armpit. This point is abbreviated **UA**

Under the Breast : Below the breast in line with the nipple. This point is abbreviated **UB**

Karate Chop: It is located in the middle of the fleshy part on the outside of the hand between the top of the wrist bone and the base of the little finger. It is abbreviated **KC**

The abbreviations for these points are summarized below in the same order as given above.

KC = Karate Chop
EB = Beginning of the Eye Brow
SE = Side of the Eye
UE = Under the Eye
UN = Under the Nose
CH = Chin
CB = Beginning of the Collar Bone
UA = Under the Arm
UB = Under the Breast
KC = Karate Chop

Whilst tapping on these points repeat the statement you have created. If you feel yourself drawn to add extra words or different statements, you can do this as long as you keep the statement in its full format. Only when you repeat rounds of the tapping would you shorten it.

Across the page is an illustration of the approximate placing of the main points minus the karate chop on the side of the hand.

Use details above to help find exact location or see a short video I have created to help at the link below:

https://tinyurl.com/y88o9ylo

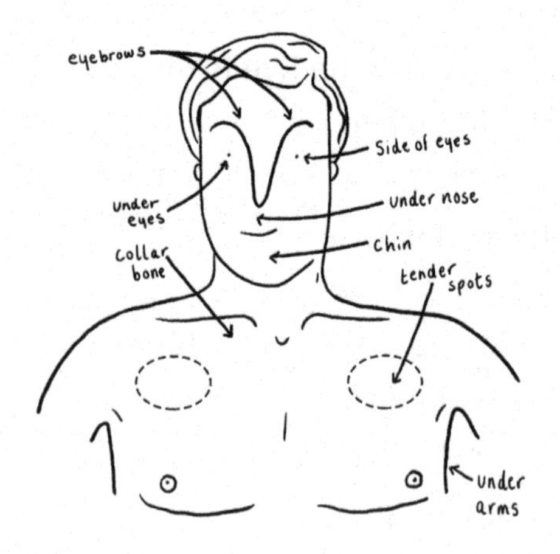

The statement is:

Even though I have this (describe the problem) I deeply and completely accept myself.

Before you begin tapping decide on a scale of 10 to 0, 10 being the highest imaginable, what is the score you would give to your pain, phobia, fear, craving, sadness, dis-comfort in this moment? 0 Is completely calm, pain free, tranquil, relaxed and happy and 10 is intense and uncomfortable.

Keep tapping until you reduce this to a low number or 0.

For more traumatic deep hurts you may need to use the extended version of EFT. This is the above version with extra points added on the end. These are:

Thumb: On the outside edge of your thumb at a point even with the base of the thumbnail.

Index Finger: On the side of your index finger (the side facing your thumb) at a point even with the base of the fingernail.

Middle Finger: On the side of your middle finger (the side closest to your thumb) at a point even with the base of the fingernail.

Little Finger: On the inside of your little finger (the side closest to your thumb) at a point even with the base of the fingernail.

The Gamut: It is on the back of either hand and is 1/2 inch behind the midpoint between the knuckles at the base of the ring finger and the little finger. If you draw an imaginary line between the knuckles at the base of the ring finger and little finger and consider that line to be the base of an equilateral triangle whose other sides converge to a point (apex) in the direction of the wrist, then the gamut point would be located at the apex of the triangle.

The purpose of the extended version is to "fine tune" the brain via some eye movements and some humming and counting.

Through connecting nerves, certain parts of the brain are stimulated when the eyes are moved. Likewise the right side of the brain (the creative side) is engaged when you hum a song and the left side (the digital side) is engaged when you count.

First tap out the beginning sequence. Instead of coming back to the Karate Chop, tap on the fingers described above while still saying your statement.

Next find the Gamut spot and begin tapping there. While there:

1. Close your eyes.
2. Open your eyes.
3. Look with your eyes hard down right while holding the head steady.
4. Look with your eyes hard down left while holding the head steady.
5. Roll your eyes in a circle as though your nose is at the centre of a clock and you are trying to see all the numbers in order.
6. Same as 5 only reverse the direction in which you roll your eyes.
7. Hum 2 seconds of a song (suggest Happy Birthday but it can be anything - usually jolly).
8. Count rapidly from 1 to 5.
9. Hum 2 seconds of a song again.

Go back to the Karate Chop and say the statement:

I deeply and completely love and accept this person I call myself, this person called (your name), myself.

This is my own unique version of an end statement that I find to be effective as it includes your name. However, if you want the original version, consult Gary Craig's website given above.

Subsequent Round Adjustments

Sometimes further rounds are required especially if your subconscious mind is holding you back from succeeding without your knowledge.

To combat this you can add:

Even though ***I still have some of this*** *(describe the problem), I deeply and completely accept myself.*

Please note the emphasized words (still & some) and how they change the thrust of the affirmation toward the remainder of the problem. It should be easy to make this adjustment.

Even though *I still have some of this fear of public speaking*, I deeply and completely accept myself.

Even though *I still have some of this headache*, I deeply and completely accept myself.

Enhancing Positive Affirmations

EFT can also be used to enhance positive affirmations: Instead of the set up statement you can state your affirmation as it is written:

I am confident, happy, vibrant and abundant

I am approved of by all of life. All is Well. I am safe

I am the love and beauty in life in full expression

Every time I hit the ball, it goes exactly where I want it

I am successful at everything I do.

Tips for Positive Statements

1. **You must want it**. Not something you feel you should do
2. **You must believe it is realistically possible.** Big enough to be exciting but small enough to be in your belief system.
3. **State your affirmation in the first person**. Present tense – EG. I am abundant not I will be abundant.
4. **State your wants and not your don't wants**. I want to be happy and healthy not I don't want to be sad and unhealthy anymore.

Appendix 3 - Chakras

Within the body there are energy centres known as chakras in which energy flows through.

Blocked energy in your chakras can often lead to illness so it is important to understand what each chakra represents and what we can do to keep this energy flowing freely.

Below is a link to a meditation that you can use to help you open your chakras and unblock them. You may like to read through the summary of each chakra below that before doing it to give you a greater understanding of how each chakra works with you:

https://tinyurl.com/yay4uzr5

Below is a summary of 7 of the main chakra's you may like to work with to help with your wellbeing:

Base Chakra

The Base Chakra represents your connection to all that is earthly giving you material and emotional support, otherwise known as grounding.

If this chakra becomes blocked it can affect your feelings around security, your financial and material wellbeing and your health.

Usually there is some kind of fear around survival if healing is required.

The Base Chakra is located:

In the base of your spine in the tailbone area.

If you are visual, when you close your eyes this chakra is usually seen as red.

Exercises that may Assist Healing:

Meditation - bring in white light around the base chakra and ask for Archangel Raphael to help heal any blocks - see **Appendix 4** on Angels for more information.

To feel grounded, stomp your bare feet on the ground.

Kundalini Yoga can help to open your lower spine - also the Bridge pose is excellent for this. Seek professional help when learning these exercises.

Hematite Stone is a good crystal for grounding. It will help to eliminate any negative energy from the body.

Hugging trees can be grounding - ask to connect to the heart of the tree when you hold your arms around it. Notice the energy exchange - if you cant just know it exists and enjoy the experience.

EFT - write out some statements for any blocks you have in this area. Tap out the sequence until you notice yourself feeling emotionally calmer when you think of these issues. Add to the statements if more ideas come.

Foods that may help with Healing:

Foods that are red such as apples and strawberries
Root vegetables such as potatoes, carrots, turnips etc.
Animal proteins such as red meat and eggs

Sacral Chakra

The Sacral Chakra relates to friendships, sexuality, life changes and abundance.

If this chakra is blocked you will experience issues around your friendships, sexuality, accepting change, difficulty in finding joy, your ability to be creative and a lack of feeling abundant.

The Sacral Chakra is located:

In the lower abdomen about 2 inches below the navel and 2 inches in.

If you are visual, when you close your eyes this chakra is usually seen as orange.

Exercises that may Assist Healing:

Meditation - bring in white light around Sacral Chakra and ask for Archangel Chamuel or Uriel in particular to help you - see **Appendix 4** on Angels for more information.

EFT - write out some statements for any blocks you have in this area. Tap out the sequence until you notice yourself feeling emotionally calmer when you think of these issues. Add to the statements if more ideas come.

Physical exercise might include pelvic thrusts and the Cobra yoga pose - ensure you get the proper advice first from a professional before attempting these moves.

Foods that may help with Healing:

Orange coloured foods such as tangerines, oranges, carrots, apricots and pumpkin etc. Drink plenty of water to help clear toxins

Solar Plexus Chakra

The Solar Plexus Chakra represents how you see yourself and how confident you are in controlling your own life. It covers your self worth, self confidence, self esteem, self value and self beliefs.

If this chakra is blocked you will be experiencing lack of confidence, low self esteem, lack of self worth, low self belief and trust in you.

The Solar Plexus Chakra is located:

In your upper abdomen in the stomach area just above your belly button.

If you are visual, when you close your eyes this chakra is usually be seen as yellow.

Exercises that may Assist Healing:

Meditation - bring in white light around the solar plexus chakra and ask for Archangel Chamuel or Jophiel in particular to help you - see **Appendix 4** on Angels for more information.

EFT - write out some statements for any blocks you have in this area. Tap out the sequence until you notice yourself feeling emotionally calmer when you think of these issues. Add to the statements if more ideas come.

Some crystals that can help are:

- Sunstone crystals help to boost your confidence and find hidden talents.
- Moonstone crystals help to heal fears and phobias.
- Amethyst crystals help to release negative energy from negative thoughts and beliefs.

Physical exercises that may help healing include Kundalini Yoga, particularly the Boat pose.

Also dancing, shaking your hips.

Foods that may help with Healing:

Yellow coloured foods like corn, yellow lentils, bananas, yellow peppers

Grains and fibre like granola and whole wheat bread that take longer to digest giving you energy for longer

Avoid processed foods especially cane sugar

Heart Chakra

The Heart Chakra represents your ability to love.

If this chakra is blocked you will be experiencing difficulties in loving you, relationships, letting go of past hurts, lack of inner peace.

The Heart Chakra is located:

In the centre of your chest just above the heart.

If you are visual, when you close your eyes this chakra is usually seen as green or pink.

Exercises that may Assist Healing:

Meditation - bring in white light around the heart chakra and ask for Archangel Chamuel or Raphael or Raguel in particular to help you - see **Appendix 4** on Angels for more information.

EFT - write out some statements for any blocks you have in this area. Tap out the sequence until you notice yourself feeling emotionally calmer when you think of these issues. Add to the statements if more ideas come.

Rose Quartz is a particularly healing crystal to help with self-love. Having a piece with you to connect to each day to help you open your heart will help to heighten your focus on love.

Physical exercise that may help is Bikram Yoga - it is yoga done in the heat, helping the blood flow more freely and detoxifying the body.

Foods that may help with Healing:

Green coloured foods such as spinach, kale, watercress, apples, kiwi, broccoli etc. Green tea is a great antioxidant

Throat Chakra

The Throat Chakra represents your ability to communicate and express yourself.

If this is blocked you will experience problems with expressing your feelings, being unable to speak your truth, allowing others to control you, holding on to secrets that need to be shared in order to be healed.

It may be that you find it difficult to speak in public.

The Throat Chakra is located:

Within your throat.

If you are visual, when you close your eyes this chakra is usually seen as blue.

Exercises that may Assist Healing:

Meditation - bring in white light around the Throat Chakra and ask for Archangel Michael or Metatron or Gabriel in particular to help you - see **Appendix 4** on Angels for more information.

EFT - write out some statements for any blocks you have in this area. Tap out the sequence until you notice yourself feeling emotionally calmer when you think of these issues. Add to the statements if more ideas come.

Blue Kyanite is a great crystal for helping with the throat chakra. Also generally any blue crystals. Wearing one around the throat area will help to loosen the negative energy stored there, releasing the blocks.

Be prepared to speak out as you have never heard yourself before if you work on this chakra.

Physical exercises that may help this chakra are shoulder stands, which help to open up the throat area. Also singing and chanting as these energetically lift the area concerned.

Foods that may help with Healing:

Blue foods such as blueberries, Concord blue grapes, plums and some sweet potatoes

Also fruits that grow on trees are meant to be true to themselves, deciding when to drop such as apples, plums, apricots, mangoes, pears etc.

Third Eye Chakra

The Third Eye Chakra represents your intuition and ability to see insights, use of your imagination, ability to tap into your inner wisdom and the skill to think and make decisions

This chakra is blocked if you are having difficulty finding direction in your life, are feeling stagnant and unable to see new opportunities, feeling disconnected, lack the ability to decide on important decisions.

Also if you are having difficulty in seeing signs from the angels working on this chakra will help.

The Third Eye is located:

On your forehead between the eyes.

If you are visual, when you close your eyes this chakra is often seen as Indigo/purple

Exercises that may be Healing:

Meditation - bring in white light around the Third Eye Chakra and ask for Archangel Raphael or Raziel or Uriel in particular to help you - see **Appendix 4** on Angels for more information.

EFT - write out some statements for any blocks you have in this area. Tap out the sequence until you notice yourself feeling emotionally calmer when you think of these issues. Add to the statements if more ideas come.

Quartz crystals and Amethyst are great for helping to open your third eye. Try putting a small piece on your forehead when you lie down and meditate. Or hold a piece in your hands.

Physical exercises that may help with healing are yoga poses such as the Child's pose and forward bends. Also eye exercises are good for clearing any negative energy around the eyes.

Foods that may be Healing:

This is a more spiritual chakra so light meals throughout the day and connection through meditation first thing in the morning before eating will be the most effective.

Also purple foods may help such as grapes, plums and beetroot.

Crown Chakra

The Crown Chakra represents our ability to connect to the universe and those who are unseen around us. It relates to inner and outer beauty and a sense of inner peace.

If this chakra is blocked you will feel unsupported, disconnected, disharmonious and unbalanced

There are other more spiritual chakras that you can connect to once you have become comfortable with connecting to your crown. You can find out more about these on the Internet or in relevant books.

The Crown Chakra is located:

On the very top of your head.

If you are visual, when you close your eyes this chakra is often seen as white or violet.

Meditation - bring in white light around your crown chakra and ask for Archangel Metatron or Jophiel in particular to help you - see **Appendix 4** on Angels for more information.

EFT - write out some statements for any blocks you have in this area. Tap out the sequence until you notice yourself feeling emotionally calmer when you think of these issues. Add to the statements if more ideas come.

Amethyst and Clear Quartz are both suitable crystals for helping you when connecting to your crown chakra. Place one in your hand when meditating to help enhance your connection.

Physical exercise that may help is running or cardio. These assist your body's energy flow, as a result clearing away toxicity.

Fresh air and a connection to nature and all things natural are most likely to help enhance your connection via your crown chakra.

Having an open mind, allowing you to explore new and unlimited possibilities will also help widen what is possible.

It is always good to express that you only wish to connect to those within the light, if wanting to connect with angels and spiritual beings.

Appendix 4 - Angels

What Are Angels?

Angels are beings of light who respond to your calls for guidance, assistance, protection, and comfort. God's thoughts of love create angels. Angels are here to help you, especially when your intent is to bring joy and healing to the world. You can ask for as many angels as you want to surround you. Ask for angels to surround your loved ones, your home, and your business. An angel's purpose is to share light and so it is their pleasure to help you. Showing appreciation by saying thank you is all they ask for in return.

The energy of an angel is pure light. It is a state of being that is all seeing whose intention is only to bring goodness and joy into your life. As you imagine heaven to be perfect and full of beauty, an angel is also this. They are filled with hope of peace and love and will make you feel special and loved if you connect to them in a pure way. Angels love to sing and play. They love to join in where laughter and joy can be found.

Guardian Angels

Everyone has a guardian angel, with no exceptions. Your guardian angel stays with you constantly, from birth until your transition back to heaven. Their love for you is unconditional and far greater than anything you will ever experience on this earth. They ensure you are always guided and kept as safe from harm as they are able.

Below is a link to a meditation helping you connect to your Guardian Angel. See meditation section on how to meditate first if you are unsure:

https://tinyurl.com/yd7zokwd

Archangels

Archangels are the keepers of the angelic realm. They organise help to where it is needed and bring information to those who request it.

These higher beings have each earned their place to be at the side of God and have been granted an aspect of the consciousness to specialise in.

Some of these Archangels have lived upon the earth and so have come to understand the challenges that humans face. This has heightened their awareness and knowledge, allowing them to have empathy with those who need it.

Archangels can be invoked simply by reciting their name. They are omnipresent and only need an invitation to be by your side.

Everything that you create is about the intention that you create it with. Working with the Archangels for matters of the light will help to enhance the work you are doing and bring new insights to you that you may not have gained otherwise.

There are many different Archangels. Below are some of the most commonly known ones together with a few basic details about them:

Archangel Michael - He who is like God

The main things Michael is known to help with are:

Commitment and dedications to one's beliefs, courage, direction, energy and vitality, life's purpose, all aspects of, motivation, protection, space clearing, releasing spirit, worthiness and increased self esteem.

Michael specialises in releasing old negative thoughts, attachments and anything you feel is holding you back.

Michael is a vibrant and fun loving angel who will help you to bring out the lighter side of you. By offering protection, Michael helps you to let go of your fears and to focus on all that is light. There is no doubt that there are few that are more powerful than he. Know that with him at your side it is much easier to be free.

Archangel Raphael - God Heals or God has Healed

The main things Raphael is known for helping with are;

Addictions and cravings, eliminating and reducing, clairvoyance, eyesight, physical and spiritual, healers, guidance and support for, healing humans and animals, pets - retrieving, lost, space clearing, releasing spirit, travellers - relating to protection, orderliness and harmony.

Raphael is a kind healer who has spent many years of his life enhancing his skills. By connecting with him you will begin to find peace within yourself creating clearer energies, giving you the potential to help more people during your lifetime. To connect with Raphael, ask for him to step forward and help you in whatever it is you are doing at that time. Begin your request with thank you. This gives the intention that your request has already been met.

Archangel Metatron - A divider and fixer of boundaries

The main things Metatron is known for helping with are:

Attention Deficit Disorder (ADD) or Attention Deficit Hyperactivity Disorder (ADHD), children's issues, recordkeeping and organisation, spiritual understanding, writing.

Metatron's energy is strong and very focused. He is highly motivated and will help you to overcome procrastination. He oversees the Akashic Records. These hold all the details of your soul's journey so far.

Archangel Uriel - God is Light

The main things Uriel is known for helping with are:

Alchemy, divine magic, earth changes, problem solving, spiritual understanding, studies, tests and students, weather, writing.

Simply call his name and Uriel will wave his magic wand upon your problem. He is willing and waiting to give advice whenever it is required. Know that sometimes help from an outside source can aid you in your studies and learning. When you are questioning the meaning of life, Uriel will help lead you to the answers that will help you most at that time.

Uriel can be a little mischievous and like all angels loves to laugh and have fun.

Archangel Chamuel - He who sees God

The main things Chamuel is known for helping with are:

Peaceful relationships, Bringing soul mates together, helps individuals attain inner peace even during turbulent times, will help you to find lost things, gives guidance in your career, life purpose, world peace.

Chamuel helps to build long lasting relationships. He is very kind, loving and sweet and will often leave you with the feeling of butterflies in your stomach when he is near. You will also often be drawn to the colour pink to reassure you of his presence.

Archangel Ariel - Lion or Lioness of God

The main things Ariel is known to help with are:

Divine magic, environmental issues especially concerning water bodies, manifestation, wild animals, fish and birds - healing and protecting them, oversees fairies and nature angels.

Ariel will normally appear with lions and is associated with the wind. If you choose to help Ariel with environmental issues you may find yourself rewarded with wonderful manifestations and increased magical power to help.

Archangel Azrael - Whom God Helps

The main things Azrael is known to help with are:

Death and bereavement, grief where there is an ending, helps those helping others with death, helps mediums that bring through messages, help spirit cross over

If you are going through any kind of grieving process, you have lost someone to the spirit world or you are helping others through death, Azrael will be by your side. Call on him and he will come. Trust and know he is there.

Archangel Sandalphon - Keeper of the Earth

The main things Sandalphon is known to help with are:

Prayers between humans and God, helps determine the gender of an unborn child, acts as a patron to musicians – will bring help to musicians when requested, helps with your connection to God.

Sandalphon's main role is to carry people's prayers to heaven. It is said because he is so tall he can reach from earth to heaven. His messages are often soft and gentle and if you are not quiet enough in the mind, you may not hear him.

Archangel Gabriel - God is my strength

The main things Gabriel is known to help with are:

Pregnancy, birth and communication, working with Mother Mary guiding conceptions, births, pregnancies, adoptions and the raising of children, helps journalists and those writing, mentors those wishing to help children, teachers, counsellors, writers, artists and actors can all ask for help from Gabriel in their careers. Gabriel will often push them along their careers when they hesitate.

Gabriel guides hopeful parents towards child conception or through the process of adopting a child. She gives them strength and courage. Gabriel also helps anyone whose life purpose involves art or communication. Gabriel will help to open doors to help you express your talent in a big way.

Archangel Raguel - Friend of God

The main things Raguel is known to help with are:

Orderliness, fairness, justice and harmony, manages relationships between humans and angels, helps harmonise relationships – brings, peace, calm and forgiveness between people, helps to heal misunderstandings, can also help you to attract wonderful friends who treat you with respect and integrity.

Known as the angel of hope, Raguel can help bring harmony to situations that have become difficult. If you are having difficulty within any kind of relationship, ask Archangel Raguel to help:

"Thank you Archangel Raguel for being by my side and helping me with this situation with (name of person struggling with). I know with the help of your strength, love and kindness, this situation will resolve itself harmoniously."

You can choose to work beside any of the Archangels that you find to be in line with the work you do. They will assist you and make you aware of tools that will help others. Some people have chosen an Archangel before ascending to the Earth. It will become apparent to you when you connect with them if this is the case.

You may have heard the name of an Archangel mentioned to you many times, but haven't yet spent the time connecting with them. When you do, you may become aware of past history that you have with them or of a specific purpose that is linked to gifts that you hold that the Archangel can help you to unleash.

These Archangels are not here to be worshipped or attached to. They are merely instruments that you can use to help you with your daily routine when needed, or to assist in times of crisis. There is no limit to their availability. They are never too busy to help. They are aspects of love as part of the consciousness as a whole and as such can be invoked whenever needed.

Some people may be privileged to see a higher being in their mediations or around them or others when they are intentionally invoking them. This is not because they are more powerful, but simply that the angel feels it necessary to show their presence in this moment. The way people visualise them will be different and based on their own perception and understanding of the spirit world.

Angels and Archangels are not in solid form like humans and so can transform into whatever version of proof that is needed. Sometimes it may just be a flash of colour that is required to confirm their presence.

How will Angels they connect with you?

Angels have many ways of reaching you. The more you spend time in the silence becoming aware of them, the more you will gain from your connection with them.

Meditation is often a great way to connect. There are many led meditations that guide you towards specific angels. You can also set an intention to meet an angel in your mind before entering the meditation.

To connect with angels, you can ask to do this whenever you wish. They will each have different ways to communicate with you. Getting to know them helps you therefore to identify this so that you can decide which resonates mostly with you at the time of needing them.

Below is a meditation you can try. It is important to set time aside for this exercise when you are unlikely to be disturbed. Allow about 1 hour.

Meditation for you to try:

Sit in a comfortable chair, close your eyes, and gently let go of all the stresses and strains of your day. Allow your mind to open up your base chakra and crown chakra. With your base chakra, ground yourself to the earth. With your crown chakra, ask to be open to universal knowledge. (The base chakra is located at the base of your spine and is often seen as the colour red. The crown chakra is based on the top of your head and is often seen as white. To open them imagine the colour in the area described and see it begin to open like a flower).

Imagine yourself entering a magical garden through a gate, full of nature and all the plants and animals that you love. Create this space. Find yourself within it a place for you to sit. Ask for your guardian angel or an angel, whichever you prefer, to step forward to you at this time. If you are not visual in your meditations, ask them to reveal a colour to you that may represent them. If you have a particular issue you would like to discuss with them, this is the time to do so. Or you can simply sit together and see how the energy feels.

Notice if any parts of the body are showing anything to you – such as a gentle brushing on the skin, or goose bumps, or a heavy or light feeling in your tummy. Ask the angel to show you how they will communicate with you.

Once you have spent as long as you wish, say goodbye to your angel and begin walking out of the garden, closing the gate behind you so that this becomes your own secret place to meet.

Close your base chakra and crown chakra before coming back into the room. (Imagine them becoming still once more).

Rub your hands together and place your palms over your eyes so that you can adjust back to the light in the room when coming back.

Below are the usual ways you might expect to receive information from your angels:

Clairaudience – The Gift of Hearing

You may hear a soft message whispered in your ear. It would feel as if you were tuned into a radio – sometimes it will be loud if it is urgent so you should hear it. Or it may be soft and gentle guiding you gently into whatever it is you are doing.

It may appear as if it is a thought - connecting to the thought and trusting its source will give you the confidence to know its authenticity.

You may hear your name mentioned.

You may hear a song tune in your head and begin to sing it or hum it.

You may hear a bell like note.

Clairvoyance – The Gift of Seeing

You may be shown an image of something that will have some meaning to you. If you don't understand it after pondering on it, ask to be shown it a different way or observe things around you.

You may also receive dreams that will be showing you images of things that may happen or help you to understand a situation that you are involved in.

Clairsentience – The Gift of Feeling

You may feel the presence of someone around you - sometimes a soft brushing against your face or a gentle push from behind.

You may also have a strong gut feeling when something is wrong or right. This will often be accentuated by your angel to help steer you in the right direction.

You may receive a warm sensation, which usually means that you are on the right path.

You may get goose bumps on your body, which is a strong sign that something is in need of consideration.

You may see things through feeling – be aware of a visualisation but instead of seeing it with your eyes, you sense it as energy.

You are likely to be very sensitive to energy with this type of gift and so will be hyper sensitive when around others, picking up negative and positive energies very quickly.

Clair cognizance – The Gift of Knowing

This is a deep understanding of a situation. Almost like a download from God giving you the solution to a problem in your mind.

This can come to you as insights that not only help you in your life but also others around you.

With this deep understanding it helps you to see through problems quickly and to find solutions from a different perspective to that which has already been expressed.

Each of these gifts is within everyone. However, it is likely that you will prefer one or two to the others and therefore these will dominate the way you receive your information.

Those in the spirit world will test out different ways to see which way you respond to most. After all they want to get their messages through. As you have free will, you have the freedom to choose how you wish to work with them, whether you decide consciously or subconsciously. They will therefore be guided by your responses.

With these four methods, if you practice working with angels on a regular basis, they will often have a more preferential way of working with you based on your own gifts. However, it is not uncommon for you to experience all four.

Other ways of Receiving Messages

Through Books, Magazines, Television, Internet

You may find yourself drawn towards certain books, magazine articles, information on the internet or programmes on the television that bring you the answer you have been looking for. This is often orchestrated by your guardian angel.

Through a Friend or Colleague or even a Stranger

Sometimes someone close to you or even a stranger will suddenly give you an answer or information that will be in response to something you have asked. Your higher self will often guide you towards these people. You might suddenly decide you need to meet up with a friend, or start talking to someone on the bus or even pick up the telephone and start chatting to him or her without really knowing why you are doing so.

The main thing is to be aware when it does and to give thanks to the angels when it happens.

In the book - The Magic of Your Mind - the power of your mind and what you are capable of is described in more detail with a chapter relating to connecting with those in spirit form. This can be found on:

http://www.aspire2bfree.com

Appendix 5 - Crystals

Below is merely a taste of what crystals are and what they can do. If you want to know more there are many experts in this field. One local to me is Judy Hall who has written numerous books on the subject.

What are Crystals?

Crystals are a gift from the earth to help with healing. They are naturally formed within the earth out of mineral solutions or gases from the molten core. These take eons to create and it is often many years before they are discovered, if ever.

Some have been manufactured in laboratories through known processes.

Each crystal is made of energy just like you. Their energy is unique to them and often has a particular purpose in helping mankind and the earth in healing areas of negativity.

Over the years many crystals have been farmed for their beauty and high net worth. This has caused a surplus of crystals to emerge that at some point will create a disharmony with the earth if nothing is given back to the earth in return.

Treating crystals with respect and using them for their purpose and returning them to the earth for recharging and replenishment is one way to achieve this.

What can they be used for?

Crystals have many uses. Some purposes include:

- Protection from negativity
- Healing of your well being
- Encouraging personal growth
- Healing of water bodies
- Relief from stress
- Relaxation
- Letting go of past hurts
- Attracting love into your life

Different types of Crystals and their uses

This is a simple guide. Please consult with a specialist in this area for further details.

- **Aventurine** – helps to re-enforce decisiveness It can improve leadership qualities. Also good for calming anxiety and fears
- **Agate** – All round healer. Particularly good for healing painful conditions such as bruises, sprains and strains
- **Amethyst** helps clear negativity, aids creativity, opens your spiritual awareness and can help with insomnia
- **Angelite** – aids your connection with angels
- **Aquamarine** – Soothing phobias and creates calmness
- **Black Tourmaline, Obsideon, Red Tigers Eye , Hermatite** – are all good for grounding and protection

- **Blue Lace Agate** – improves courage and trust. Also known for helping to strengthen bones
- **Carnelian** - Helps with fear of death and grief from death. Also motivates success in business.
- **Citrine** – Great to help with well-being - Good to assist with depression and relieving negative thinking. Also a prosperity stone.
- **Diamond** - Helps bring harmony and strength to relationships, helps bring fearlessness and purity of mind - aids glaucoma
- **Fluorite** – Helps with relaxation especially where there is stress. Also good for negating colds
- **Garnet** – Helps to alleviate effects of trauma
- **Hematite** – Increases self belief - also good for blood flow - helps to strengthen boundaries
- **Howlite** - Known to help eliminate anger giving a calming effect. Also good for teeth and bones.
- **Lapis Lazuli** – Protection from physical danger encouraging honesty and integrity - good for helping with friendships
- **Malachite** – Transformational stone helping you through change
- **Moonstone** – Encourages femininity, aids pregnancy
- **Quartz** - Aids channelling and healing. Also good to help disperse negative energies

- **Ruby** – Detoxes the body, helping to relieve anger and negativity - good to help prevent psychic attacks. Also great for the heart chakra.
- **Rose quartz** – helps with self-love, past hurts of the heart, brings harmony to relationships. Can assist sleep and alleviate stress.
- **Sapphire** - Helps to remove toxins from the body
- **Sodalite** – Helps to clear the mind of negativity and bring joy. Also helps your metabolism.
- **Tiger's eye** – Known as 'the confidence stone' it can increase your confidence. Also helps your digestive system.
- **Turqurenite** - Used to help stimulate passion and heart energy. Also used for healing chills and fevers.

Appendix 6 - Affirmations

When your subconscious mind is filled with negative data it can be hard to break the habit of producing negative feelings and thoughts.

Using affirmations can help to re-programme your mind. Each affirmation can be used to trick the mind into believing something different from your reality until the thought becomes so embedded it becomes your new way of being.

The affirmation is used to confirm that a feeling or thought is real. Your intention behind it therefore needs to match the vibration you wish to create.

For example, you could say, I am open to receive wealth and abundance in my life. If however, you are not willing to do anything positive towards this, it might take more than an affirmation to make it real.

If you repeat something often enough, eventually the mind does not know the difference between what is real and what is not. It will begin to believe you and accept that what you say is the truth.

The mind takes instructions from you. This is why your thoughts are so important since it is these that inform the mind how to respond to situations before you.

If you are unaware of your thoughts you have no way of taking control of your life as your mind will keep on repeating old patterns that are imprinted into your way of being.

You can use affirmations in any area of your life to make improvements within it.

Below are a few ideas for affirmations relating to different areas of your life:

Affirmations for Health

Every day in every way I am getting healthier and healthier and feeling better and better

I love myself and I am perfectly healthy

Every cell in my body is health conscious. I am a health freak

I am full of energy and vitality and my mind is calm and peaceful

Affirmations for Relationships

I deserve to be loved

I am open to receive a loving relationship into my life

I love unconditionally without judgment or expectation

I share love with others easily and freely

I find loving and supportive friendships and relationships easy to manifest

Affirmations for Abundance

My world is filled with love, abundance and happiness

I deserve abundance and prosperity

I manifest abundance with my unique gifts and talents

I live a joyful honest and fulfilled life

I deserve to live a complete and full life

I produce financial abundance doing what I love

How to use them

It is best to repeat the affirmation chosen at least three times each time that you use it. To embed it even deeper, you might also like to tap on the EFT points as you say each one.

Saying them to yourself when you first wake up, around lunchtime and in the evening before going to bed will help to implant them strongly into your mind.

The more you do this, the greater the chance of changing your vibration to match what is being said.

You will begin to notice small changes within yourself gradually over the coming months' as these new thoughts become your new reality.

May your journey onwards
Be filled with love

Contact Details

Visit Sarah at
http://www.aspire2bfree.com
and
http://theangelwhisperer.co.uk

Join Sarah on Twitter at
http://twitter.com/aspire2bfree

Discover other titles by Sarah Haywood at
https://Smashwords.com

Lightning Source UK Ltd.
Milton Keynes UK
UKOW01f0348260717
306061UK00002B/209/P